Dancing With

COPYRIGHT © Dr. Danny Griffin,
1st Edition August 2018
Printed in the United States of America

Dr. Danny Griffin
dwadegriffin@gmail.com
www.SpiritualMaintenance.org

Danny Griffin's books are available at special quantity discounts to use as premiums or sales promotions, or for use in training/teaching programs. To place a bulk order, please contact dwadegriffin@gmail.com.

Cover images used by permission Copyright: denisovd/123RF Stock Photo

Table of Contents

DEDICATION

This is another book dedicated to my dear faithful wife Diane and my youngest daughter, Elizabeth, who have endured my many hours of writing and rewriting as I worked through my own desire to be real in dealing with the hurts and joys of life. I also dedicate this book to Grace Fellowship and those special people who daily share accountability on our journey.

SPECIAL APPRECIATION

I offer very special thanks to those who have helped me in this labor of love.

I thank Sue Ellen Grant for re-typing my manuscript and Donnie Cleveland for his work with our website. He has faithfully attended to its development and now maintains it.

A special thanks to John and Susan Heiermann for their creative genius and faithfulness in giving life to my books.

Finally I thank my friend, Ron McRay, an accomplished writer of many books for his editing help.

INTRODUCTION

Jesus said,

> *They are like unto children sitting in the marketplace, and calling one to another, and saying, We have piped unto you, and you have not **DANCED**; we have mourned to you, and you have not wept. For John the Baptist came neither eating bread nor drinking wine; and you say, He hath a devil. The Son of man is come eating and drinking; and you say, Behold a gluttonous man, and a winebibber, a friend of publicans and sinners!*
> **Luke 7:32-34**

We are living in a world of increasing conflict and confusing ideologies. As believers in the Lord Jesus Christ our lifestyle is to reveal God's love and grace at work in us. It is more about the walk than talk. Thus we desire to be flexible, listening to others who struggle and **HURT** on their journey. As believers we are not salesmen but **AMBASSADORS**. Our greatest joy is representing God's grace in a natural hurting world and culture. We have no product to sell but are receivers of God's love and grace. Our lifestyle daily presents us an opportunity to be a witness, not a salesman. Allowing us to walk and listen (**DANCE)** with compassion, for others who **HURT!**

FOREWORD

JESUS DECLARED, "COME UNTO ME ALL YOU THAT ARE BURDENED AND WEARY AND I WILL GIVE YOU REST".

Scripture declares, "BEAR ONE ANOTHER'S **BURDENS** AND THUS FULFILL THE LAW OF CHRIST".

King DAVID declared of the LORD, "YOU HAVE TURNED MY CRYING INTO **DANCING** AND MY CLOTHES OF SADNESS INTO **GLADNESS**".

DANCING WITH JESUS IN A HURTING WORLD IS ABOUT OUR DAILY WALK TOGETHER IN A BROKEN WORLD. THE GOOD NEWS IS THAT JESUS DIED ON THE CROSS, WAS BURIED, THEN ROSE FROM THE DEAD FOR YOU AND ME!

IS JESUS A LIAR, A LUNATIC, OR LORD?

C.S. LEWIS a former atheist who became a believer, introduced me to these options in his writings years ago. JESUS found me at a very "NEEDY" time in my journey. I not only needed a different DANCE but a different DANCE PARTNER. The chapters of this book share my TRUTH JOURNEY that empowered me to move from ME-SUS to JESUS! All of us confront our PAST, our PAIN, BROKEN DREAMS, AND BROKEN HEARTS along with life's PRESSURES and PROBLEMS producing HURTS that NO other human can fix or heal.

YOU ARE INVITED TO DANCE WITH ME AS I DANCE WITH JESUS IN THIS HURTING WORLD!

Danny Griffin / player-coach
Director of Spiritual Maintenance Ministries
Charlotte, NC
Web: spiritualmaintenance.org
E-mail: dwadegriffin@gmail.com

Part 1

THE WAY

THE WAY IS FOR GOING AND EARLY BELIEVERS WERE SPOKEN OF AS "THE WAY." THE ISSUE IS WHO WILL SHOW US THE WAY? WILL IT BE RELIGION, PHILOSOPHY, GANGS, GROUPS OR GATHERINGS WHO HAVE DECIDED TO SPEAK ON OUR BEHALF? SCRIPTURE DECLARES,

"NO MAN HAS SEEN GOD AT ANYTIME: THE ONLY BEGOTTEN SON WHO IS IN THE BOSOM OF THE FATHER, (JESUS) HAS EXPLAINED HIM"!

CHAPTER 1

WHAT'S THE QUESTION?

Years ago I heard an interesting story that may be more fiction than fact; **nevertheless**, its point is valid. It seems that in a particular southern university during a week of spiritual emphasis, students had gathered to hear an outstanding guest speaker. With great enthusiasm, he proclaimed the answer to life's many issues. He finished by declaring in a dramatic manner, "**JESUS IS THE ANSWER**"!

As the story goes, there was absolute silence as the students sat spellbound by the dynamic closing remark. At that moment, from the rear of the room, came a voice speaking in broken English, "**SIR, JESUS CHRIST MAY BE THE ANSWER, BUT WHAT IS THE QUESTION?**"

We live in a world that is ever competing for our attention. We are constantly bombarded from every side with well-packaged answers for our material, physical and spiritual **well-being.** It may be that many of us, as the young man in the story, have determined that somewhere in it all, we have lost the question. As believers, we understand Jesus Christ as "the answer."

JESUS SAID,

> "I am the Way, the Truth, and the Life; no one comes to the Father but by me."

We believers are most adept at giving quick answers before a person's life has been touched by our caring. No matter how correct our answers, questions of eternal significance are raised more by truth in action—life, rather than lip. Of even greater impact is a proper balance of both.

Believer-witnesses are eager to see mankind find their way. We must never forget that the quest of mankind for God had its beginning in God's quest for mankind. It is the Father-Creator who stalks mankind seeking to bring mankind to Himself.

Jesus said,

> "For the Son of Man has come to seek and to save that which is lost."

The spiritual yearnings of mankind and their questions of eternal significance do not originate within themselves. Throughout history, the ultimate questions of life, death and eternity have originated with God. Whether in the storms of life without or the still small voice within, God has put in all mankind a monitor for His voice called conscience, which can be programed out of order.

Finally we must respond to Him on the basis of that special revelation of Himself in the person and the work of Jesus Christ "the Messiah," by which all mankind might be saved. It is the work of God alone to draw men unto Himself, and it is a person, who by the Spirit of God, believes Him who draws."

John said of this Christ,

> *"There was that true Light which, coming into the world, enlightens every man."*

God said in Genesis,

> *"My Spirit shall not always strive with man forever, because he also is flesh."*

The Apostle Paul, centuries later said,

"For the flesh sets its desire against the Spirit, and the Spirit against the flesh, for these are in opposition to one another."

This is so because of that hideous thing that entered the Garden shortly after Adam and Eve took up residence.

Paul the Apostle stated it this way,

"Through one man sin entered into the world, and death through sin."

The natural man/woman is dead in trespasses and sin and has no ears to hear. Therefore rejecting the condemnation produced by sin, that entered the world by Adam.

Again the Apostle Paul speaks,

"The natural man does not understand the things of the Spirit of God: for they are foolishness to him, and he cannot understand them, because they are spiritually understood."

It was the sin of Adam in the garden that gave birth to the natural man,

"For all have sinned…"

Mankind's greatest adversary is ourselves. We discover the enemy and it is us.

In the beginning of human salvation history we are introduced to God's first dealing with the sinfulness of mankind as manifest in Adam and Eve. Eve was deceived and Adam was willfully disobedient. The first citizens of planet Earth had discovered their hideous, fallen and rebellious nature. Gone was innocence. Guilt and condemnation reigned. This was a bittersweet moment of "first knowing" with which all can identify. It was at that point in time that Adam and Eve discovered the word "lost" with its fear and pain as they hid in the garden naked and afraid.

Into this idyllic garden came the voice of the Father in the "cool of the day." The serpent had been the voice of evil to Eve. God in creating man and woman gave them a God kind of likeness, the ability of CHOICE. The fruit of the serpent's questions corrupted by bad choices destroyed forever man's garden of fellowship and tranquility as God's overseers. The garden was filled with rebellion and disobedience.

Eve was deceived, but Adam with eyes wide open, willfully disobeyed, partaking of her deception. The Father-Creator sought them out and by doing so began building that long bridge of grace, revealing the first Gospel message. That eternal question echoes yet across the eons of time as God the Father, Creator and Redeemer first heralded that question from a broken heart in the garden to Adam and Eve, as they hid, **"WHERE ARE YOU?"**

Isaiah *spoke* Jehovah's Word as he declared,

> *"There is no other God besides Me. A righteous God and Savior; there is none except Me. Turn to me and be saved, all the ends of the earth, for I am God, and there is no other. I have sworn by Myself, the word has gone forth from My mouth in righteousness."*

It was there that the very nature of God was revealed as He, the Creator-Savior, called out to the crown of His creation. The question that was asked of Adam and Eve did not betray ignorance on the part of God the Father, but rather asking them to give an account of themselves. Thus, it was the loving Creator who gave the first gospel message and invitation, **"WHERE ARE YOU?"** A divinely asked question opens the door of understanding, and is at the heart of every redeeming answer and conclusion.

Jesus **ASKED MANY QUESTIONS!**

"Who do you say that I am?"

"What do you think about the Christ; whose son is He"?

"For what does it profit a man to gain the world and forfeit his soul"?

In answer to Simon Peter, as he declared his desire to follow Him, Jesus asked,

"Will you lay down your life for me"?

The questions of Jesus have within them the making of fruitful, life-changing answers. The Old Testament also reveals questions employed by Jehovah. God the creator knows what is in man. Thus God questions mankind, and He alone knows the answer

"Where are you"?

"Who told you that you were naked"?

"What is this you have done"?

Such questions deliver one to a moment of truth as no aggressive declaration ever could. Mankind must come to their own answers as they deal with that which is eternal and absolute. Individuals are ultimately driven into the arms of God either by truth or circumstances. All the contrived questions of mankind can never truly produce the God-man confrontation as do questions of eternal significance. Eternal questions resound from eternity to eternity and never change because God never changes, and they are the very Word of God. Adam and Eve were under the eye of God and to Him alone they answered.

Rebecca Pippert writes concerning authority and questions,

> *"We need to raise questions that deal with the source of authority. In other words, we ask why they believe what they do. Is something true for them because it subjectively 'feels right' or because of tradition they were taught or because they believe it is scientifically sound? But we must deal with each person's actual questions."*

When people do not have questions about their present position we need to listen lovingly for their cry for help. Perhaps the emphasis should not be on our asking questions but raising questions within the hearer. Human questions that demand instant answers can become pushy and intimidating. Questions demand that the mind be in gear and ready to process. There are no bad questions but we have often been given bad answers. Getting a hearing for even the right questions does not guarantee that mankind will receive truth. Fallen mankind is natured to hide or run when God begins to deal with their life.

We should pray daily that we would be faithful to opportunities to raise questions in the natural mind. Faithfully representing the truths of God's Word by our lifestyle can impact the life of the natural mind that is blinded by the god of this world.

The outreach of the **AMBASSADOR** is the work of the Spirit of God. Lewis Sperry Chafer writes concerning this truth,

> *"The convicting work of the Spirit involves a radical change in the deepest part of man's being, where his motives and desires are first formed; so that an entirely new conception of the God-provided grounds of redemption and a vision of the glorious Person of Christ are created."*

This being so, we can be absolutely certain that the building of a redemptive answer in relation to mankind's hurt and eternal salvation must come from the One who authors such salvation. Therefore it behooves us to turn our attention to the building of a base for caring as found in God's graceful quest for hurting mankind.

The Apostle Paul said it well,

> "*What then is Apollos? And what is Paul? Servants through whom you believed, even as the Lord gave opportunity to each one. I planted, Apollos watered, but God was causing the growth. So then neither the one who plants nor the one who waters is anything, but God who causes the growth. Now he who plants and he who waters are one; but each will receive his own reward according to his own labor.*"

IF JESUS IS THE ANSWER!

WHAT IS THE QUESTION?

CHAPTER 2

FRUIT OF THE LOOM

As soon as Adam and Eve fell from innocence their first and almost instinctive move was to cover themselves and hide. From that time forward, such has been evidenced in man's behavior as he deals with the disease of sin. The Scripture declares that "they knew" and then made for themselves "loin coverings."

The covering of the first couple was only the covering of physical nakedness that reflected the sense of knowing and guilt which is always the fruit of sin. To discover evil in oneself or in another is to be overwhelmed with a sense of unreality and denial that such a thing can be.

The Scriptures declare that mankind's heart is "desperately wicked, who can know it" as it is "more deceitful than all else." Because this is so, mankind seeks to hide its guilt and shame.

In the old western films of the forties, the villains dragged a tree behind their horses in an attempt to cover their tracks. Mankind's constant attempt to "cover tracks" in relation to their hurting activity and the guilt thereof is like that. We give ourselves away, as did our first parents, by that which receives the full attention of our failure.

Thus, the Scripture accounts reveal that planet Earth's original couple turned from the sufficiency of the Creator and His commands to the desires of their mind's eye and appetite. Adam and Eve had turned their eyes from the Creator to the appeal of the earthly byway of their fleshly appetites – the lust of the eyes, the lust of the flesh and the pride of life.

Scripture speaks by the Apostle John,

> *"And this is the condemnation that light is come into the world, and men loved darkness rather than light, because their deeds were evil."*

The guilt of Adam and Eve was not so much in their act but in their disobedience. By so doing, they chose listening to the voice of the serpent and self-desire rather than the command of God to not eat from the tree of "good and evil".

All sin is ultimately unbelief, which is idolatry. The immediate result of that sin was that Adam and Eve reached for a covering; and mankind ever since, in guilt and sin has done the same. They sought to cover their disobedience by the works of their own hands.

The Scriptures declare,

> *"They sewed fig leaves together and made themselves loin coverings."*

Mankind makes his own suit of righteousness, tailor-made with his own hands, "the fruit of the loom!" Since the fall, mankind has never run short of the material of "self-righteousness."

God's opinion of this common mistake to fallen mankind is revealed by Isaiah as he declares,

> *"All our righteousness is as filthy rags."*

GOD'S PROVISION was made for mankind after their feeble PERFORMANCE to clothe themselves. The Scriptures say,

> *"And the Lord God made garments of skin for Adam and his wife, and clothed them."*

The power of sin became a reality in the life of Adam and Eve. God, in His grace, instantly sought to re-introduce Himself to them. As their Creator-Father, He pursued them by manifesting His concern and love for their lives, which were broken by sin.

In so doing He did not diminish His love and grace, but only called them back from sin's unreality to the reality of His purpose and divine decrees. Then, in one great stroke of grace, He redeemed them, symbolizing it by clothing them with those garments that He provided, by shedding the garden's first blood. In so doing, He declared them "covered."

This covering was the "fruit of the womb." There is no greater picture of salvation with God tailor-making that righteousness with which He clothes those who are under the curse and condemnation of sin.

Scripture declares,

> *"Without the shedding of blood, there is no remission of sin."*

The salvation message to Adam and Eve is declared and delivered by the Creator-Father Himself. Contemporary mankind, as mankind throughout the ages, has constantly failed to understand that. Just like our original parents after the fall, we too stand condemned apart from God.

J.I. Packer says of modern man as he views his condition,

> *"Modern man is convinced that, despite all his peccadilloes – drinking, gambling, reckless driving, 'fiddling', black and white lies, sharp practice in trading, dirty reading, and what have you – he is at heart a thoroughly good fellow. Then as pagans do (and modern man's heart is pagan; make no mistake about that), he imagines God as a magnified image of himself, and assumes that God shares his own complacency about himself. The thought of himself as a creature fallen from God's image, a rebel against God's rule, guilty and unclean in God's sight, fit only for God's condemnation, never enters his head."*

Fallen mankind not only does not see themselves as sinful, they don't see themselves in need of God. They do not reach out to God; but as Adam and Eve, they clothes themselves in the "fruit of the loom," that clothing of their own making. In so doing, they feel sufficiently covered. Sin always makes naked, stripping mankind's life of purpose and meaning.

The stark reality of rebellion and evil is rampant in our society; but mankind who is ever prideful and self-sufficient, reaches for that which is convenient and self-serving. Thus, all that mankind provides for themselves is temporary and inadequate relief, which in finality is self-deception. Religion and philosophy and any other self-imposed clothing for man's psyche are but feeble efforts of self-reconstruction by which mankind hopes to be better and to be fulfilled.

These things, though not evil within themselves, become the epitome of evil when they are that by which sinful mankind attempts to put themselves right. The works of mankind, with their attempt at merit and self-righteousness, represent so well the "fig-leaves" of Adam and Eve becoming the "fruit of the loom" by which mankind attempts to cover their tracks and declare themselves "not guilty."

God the Creator, on the other hand, knows mankind's deceptions well and declares their righteousness as not existent, for the Scriptures declare,

> *"There is none righteous, not even one; there is none who understands, there is none who seeks for God; all have turned aside, together they have become useless; there is none who does good, there is not even one."*

Mankind cannot redeem themselves; they cannot cover their tracks; they cannot cover their nakedness since there is nothing hidden from God. Mankind's evil, therefore, must not and cannot be labeled as a mistake, error, miscalculation, or simple immaturity, but rather sin.

Sin is arrogance and rebellion against God. Eve fell through deception and Adam by personal choice. Their first move after the fall was to make their own covering by the "fruit of the loom." As then so it is now, a fruitless effort that is doomed from the start to fail. It could not prevent God from finding them, from judging them and justifying them by His covering. This self- effort on their part could not satisfy God and restore the brokenness nor restore mankind to their original innocence.

Isaiah of old said it this way,

> *"All we like sheep have gone astray, each of us has turned to his own way; but the Lord has caused the iniquity of us all to fall on Him."*

It was God the Father-Creator who was the first evangelist of good news to a fallen creature. It was He who declared mankind undone and guilty, cursed to endure with a fallen creation, living by the sweat of their brow, struggling ever with pain, suffering, hurt and physical death.

Salvation from the beginning was God's covering for mankind's sin and rebellion. Fallen man is impossibly undone and sinful, dead in trespasses and sin, crawling in the dust from whence he came. Without refuge or cover, has now surrendered his high and lofty place as "ruler" of sky, earth and every living thing, stands under condemnation of God. But God in His grace has redeemed His creation "by the shedding of blood" and the gift of His righteousness.

John Newton said it well when he wrote,

> *"Amazing Grace, how sweet the sound, that saved a wretch like me. I once was lost but now I'm found, was blind but now I see."*

The message is clear. The Father-Creator Himself initiated redemption's story. Drawn upon the canvas of history is the trail of blood from that first animal slain, to His "only begotten Son" who would, centuries later, perfect and complete the tapestry of salvation's truth as,

"...the lamb of God who taketh away the sin of the world."

On a cruel Roman cross, Christ died overlooking a garbage dump outside Jerusalem as His life's blood was shed for the sins of the whole world. The animal that was alive had been slain for the covering of Adam and Eve until that time was to come in its fullness and God would send forth His Son. What's it all about? The answer is obvious, the works of man versus the grace of God.

PERFORMANCE of the flesh versus the **PROVISION** of God. Works theology always says the same thing.

Man seeks to redeem himself, his society and his world by his works, deeds and methods that are expressed in thousands of different guises and forms. God the Father, the Redeemer of mankind has revealed from the beginning that mankind's righteousness and their very best effort will never be enough. It is about: GOD'S PROVISION NOT OUR PERFORMANCE!
Mankind's works can never redeem them.

"...For salvation is of the Lord"

Adam and Eve left the garden to travail and labor amidst a broken, cursed creation. A fallen order and fallen man were bound together until, in God's time, He would "restore all things." We who would share the good news of God's love and grace, must declare faithfully that God's grace has purchased a covering for all who call upon His name."

It is the Lord Christ, the Jesus of History, the author and the finisher of our salvation by faith. Only His PROVISION will satisfy. Substitutions, abridgements or any other adjustments will never satisfy.

> Salvation is forever and always: *"...by grace through faith, and that not of ourselves, it is the gift of God, not of works lest any man should boast"*

The **AMBASSADOR** lifestyles God's provision for eternal life so that others might TRUST HIM BY FAITH and be blessed.

> *"To Him who has chosen us in Himself before the foundation of the world that we might be holy and blameless before Him in love."*

CHAPTER 3

HIDE AND SEEK

The **AMBASSADOR'S** message by its very nature collides head-on with God's and mankind's redemptive struggle. God is the "seeker" and mankind, the "hidden" one, attempting to cover their tracks by their own defenses and self-righteousness.

Scripture declares,

> *"There is none who seeks after God."*

Mankind is cast in the role of villain by their own inclinations to evil which is natural to them. Without a thought we cover ourselves. When caught in our deceptions we excuse our conduct by manipulation of words and events, thus attempting to justify our meanness and cover our tracks. Mankind is so given to the deceptions of the heart that we must always "keep face" whatever the cost. Jeremiah revealed well the mind of God concerning this condition of the human heart.

> *"The heart is more deceitful than all else and is desperately sick; who can understand it"?*

The bottom line of it all, no matter how one might say it, we are all "lost", cut off from the life of God, whom we were to glorify. Evil is no greater today than in the beginning. Our technology allows it to be more devious, available and amplified to mankind.

The Westminster Catechism declares,

> *"...the chief end of man is to glorify God and to enjoy Him forever."*

JESUS declared that he had,

> *"come to seek and save that which was lost"*
>
> *"no man seeks God"*

It is obvious that "natural man" upon the stage of life, "seeks not God" as though there were no God at all.

The Apostle Paul said,

> *"The natural man does not understand the things of God for they are foolishness to him."*

Adam and Eve revealed that prototype of behavior that mankind would always exhibit without fail. In so doing Adam revealed a plan of action that was stamped indelibly upon his soul so that all mankind from that point on would repeat it.

Adam said to God,

"I heard the sound of Thee in the garden and I was afraid because I was naked; so I hid myself."

God saw Adam as a rebellious child caught in an act of disobedience. He stood under the gun of God's questioning, where he revealed an obvious trait of mankind, blaming others and denying guilt. Mankind attempts to cover their guilt and declare their innocence. Only as the Father-Creator deals with our life do we acknowledge our broken world of unreality and fantasy. It is in those moments of revelation by the Spirit of God and the Scripture that our hearts are undressed. It is then that we admit our nakedness and vulnerability. It is at this point that we are enabled to identify our game of hide and seek.

Thus Adam and Eve in such a moment covered themselves with the fig leaves of their own best effort. Hiding from whom? Fearful of what? How naked? Mankind has never been able to answer these questions. All the social and behavioral disciplines that seek to answer questions concerning mankind's behavior are ultimately thwarted and frustrated dealing with the problem of sin. They bypass it, deny it or redefine it. Only spiritual hunger and brokenness give discernment of the true disease of mankind's heart.

God offers mankind the gift of His righteousness, bringing mankind to those answers that only He can provide. The good news is that God has indeed provided the only covering for sin, the very removal of sin's penalty. Believers are never referred to as good or bad but weak or strong depending on their walk and lifestyle.

Augustine said,

> *"We were made it is true, by the hand of Truth, but because of sin we were cast forth upon days of vanity."*

It is this very fact that causes humankind so much pain and **HURT** as they seek to escape nothingness, boredom and the temporary cycles that comprise this brief life. It is in this oft-repeated cycle the contemporary person hides from the realities of the Creator. Neither caring nor dealing with these life matters brings mankind to fearing life and death, occupying themselves with multitudes of escapes and escapades.

In our daily troubling circumstances, mankind gets glimpses of our nakedness, realizing that we are vulnerable and destructible. In this lostness multitudes are unable to hear the "sound" of God in the modern garden of human brokenness. Adam and Eve heard the "sound of the Lord God walking in the garden." God has always walked among His creation. He walks today among us by His Spirit "drawing mankind to Himself" when hearing the Gospel message and responding to God's love and grace. We as believer-witnesses are committed to the ongoing of the Gospel message as God's **AMBASSADORS!** Discovering our peace in Him, we are then no longer afraid of Him who knows us and loves us!

JESUS DECLARED,

> *"My peace I give to you, not as the world gives, do I give to you. Let not your heart be troubled, let it not be fearful."*

Martin Luther speaks vividly to this point,

> *"My situation was that although an impeccable monk, I stood before God as a sinner troubled in conscience; and I had no confidence that my merit would assuage Him. Therefore, I did not love a just and angry God, but rather hated and murmured against Him. Yet, I clung to dear Paul and had a great yearning to know what he meant. Night and day I pondered until I saw the connecting between the justice of God and the statement that 'the just shall live by faith.' Then I grasped that the justice of God is that righteousness by which, through grace and sheer mercy, God justifies us through faith.*

Thereupon, I felt myself to be reborn and to have gone through open doors into Paradise. The whole of Scripture took on a new meaning, and whereas before the 'justice of God' had filled me with hate, now it became to inexpressibly sweet in greater love. This passage of Paul became to me the gate of Heaven...if you have a true faith that Christ is your Savior. Then at once you have a gracious God; for faith leads you in and opens up God's heart and will, that you should see pure grace and overflowing love. This is to behold God in faith that you should look upon His fatherly, friendly heart in which there is no anger or ungraciousness. He who sees God as angry does not see Him right, but looks only on a curtain, as if a dark cloud had been drawn across his face."

Martin Luther found love and acceptance of his person in Christ, the Messiah, as did the woman at the well of Sychar. Upon her realization of who He was she declared,

"Come see a man who told me all the things that I have done."

Gone were the hidden recesses of her inner person with all of its darkness, for the Light had come and the spontaneity of spirit as God's peace had become a reality. God in His great love wherein He loves us, seeks us out by His grace and pardons our sinful condition whereby we have peace with Him through our Lord Jesus Christ.

J.I Packer says of this grace,

> *"Grace means God's love in action is toward men who merited the opposite of love. Grace means God moving heaven and earth to save sinners who could not lift a finger to save themselves."*

CHAPTER 4

THE SOUND AND FURY

History has shown beyond a doubt that sin is a noisy and complex matter. Its fury and travesty have left the sands of time covered with broken lives and distraught souls. Their plight has not only destroyed them, but taken literally unnumbered others with them. In their wake have also gone kingdoms and nations.

The Scriptures declare,

> *"The soul that sinneth, it shall surely die"*

> *"The wages of sin is death"*

This wage of death is not just physical death. More than that, it is man's eternal disconnection from the life of God who breathed into man in the beginning the breath of life, by which he became a living soul.

The natural man/woman does not find this reality to be of any consequence to them. In the natural state, mankind does not perceive the things of God or the disaster of eternity without the gift of eternal life. Mankind, in the natural, is constantly ravaged and plagued by sin. Their existence is constantly eroded by sin, yet in their frustration with that which he does not understand or identify he is like people who constantly scratch an unknown itch. They medicate the cancer of sin which flavors their total life with concoctions that will never abate the "sound and fury" of sin. Adam and Eve revealed to us a man and woman in the throes of sin and rebellion as they hid in the garden after their disobedience.

As a youth in Florida I lived through many hurricanes and remember seeking secure shelter. The storms of life drive mankind to seek cover. The "sound and fury" of sin infects all of mankind, but without knowledge of the enemy. The natural man/woman hides themselves in shelters of their own making. At best, their places of hiding pacify them for a season. They spend their lives moving from one shelter to another, never understanding that it is their nature that is corrupt. Mankind, at best, shelters themselves in the security of their philosophies and self-improvement ideologies. They do this consistently as they travel along the road of life to their destruction.

Mankind has chosen in this generation, as in generations past, to stand in their own righteousness. They are seeking always to be the "adequate one," declaring their abilities, technology, education, wealth and standing before mankind as "covering enough."

How sad! But mankind does not in themselves perceive the truth that sin is not only the evil of <u>doing wrong</u> but the evil of <u>being wrong</u> in their standing before God.

Mankind is not declared sinners because they sin, but they sin because they are sinners by nature. Mankind is evil because of being disconnected from the life of God. Therefore, sin is not so much the presence of evil, but the absence of righteousness. Mankind in their darkness does not ever perceive that they have no light other than conscience and creation.

If that light in him is darkness, how great is the darkness? How great the condemnation is that mankind is under because they believed not. Thus, most natural men/women in their spiritual blindness acknowledge the general witness of conscience or creation only as it fits into their scheme of morality and deity. When this general witness is responded to by natural man, it is usually without redemptive meaning. It is often called religion!

Paul said concerning the Ephesians prior to their salvation,

"You were dead in your trespasses and sins."

So indeed is the indictment against all mankind, "for all have sinned."

The key truth is that,

> "...they have come short of the glory of God."

Again, as believer-witnesses, we must understand the very nature of sin as God sees it. If not, we will but fight the winds with human schemes and methods that call mankind, for a moment out of the storm, but will never anchor lives to that eternal rock.

Thomas Hastings wrote years ago,

> "Rock of Ages cleft for me,
>
> Let me hide myself in thee:
>
> Let the water and the blood,
>
> From Thy wounded side which flowed,
>
> Be of sin the double cure,
>
> Save from wrath and make me pure."

Unless this "sound and the fury" is invaded by the Spirit of God and the Word of life, there is no way that mankind's frail bark can understand or respond to God. A true witness lifestyle must deal with the problem of sin as God deals with it and proclaim that God alone has provided for the remedy of sin. Sin is, "the falling short of the glory of God," that is a refusal to acknowledge God's absolute rule and reign over mankind. This is manifest by outward rebellion or evil's inward design and disobedience.

The Apostle Paul states,

> *"Through one man sin entered into the world and death by sin, and so death spread to all men because all have sinned."*

Dietrich Bonhoeffer writes concerning man's fall and position as a sinner,

> *"The fall of man in God's creation is both inconceivable and unalterably inexcusable; and therefore the word 'disobedience' does not exhaust the facts of the case. It is revolt; it is the creature's departure from the attitude which is the only possible attitude for him; it is the creature's becoming Creator; it is defection; it is the fall from being held in creatureliness.*
>
> *This defection is a continual falling, a plunging into bottomless depths, a being relinquished, a withdrawal ever farther and deeper. And in all this, it is not simply a moral lapse but the destruction of creation by the creature. The Fall affects the whole of the created world which is henceforth plundered of its creatureliness as it crashes blindly into infinite space, like a meteor which has torn away from its nucleus. It is of this fallen-falling world that we now speak."*

Bonhoeffer has described well the "sound and fury" of mankind's fall and his resulting sinfulness. Mankind's rupture of sin is just too great to patch up with the milk of human kindness, religious reforms and a made-over society. God must do a total work whereby mankind individually might be delivered and "declared righteous" one person at a time. There is absolutely nothing in mankind – their philosophies, technology or brilliance – that could ever produce that result. The Scriptures say,

> *"All have sinned."*

Of this miserable condition St. Augustine speaks,

> *"Thus, then matters stood. The whole mass of the human race was under condemnation, was lying steeped and wallowing in misery, and was being tossed from one evil to another, and having joined the faction of the fallen angels, was paying the well-merited penalty of that impious rebellion. For whatever the wicked freely do through blind and unbridled lust, and whatever they suffer against their will in the way of open punishment, this all evidently pertains to the just wrath of God."*

It is not only reasonable, but necessary and logical that a perfect and loving Creator must at all times be absolutely just and without partiality in His judgment of all that is evil and disorderly. God placed an absolute just curse upon man, woman and serpent as well as the whole created order that fell with them. Fallen man has progressed from the quiet communion of Adam and Eve in that perfect idyllic garden where man walked in "declared innocence" to a fallen, condemned and cursed creature and creation. This indeed is the "sound and fury" of sin. To have a proper understanding of sharing the Gospel we must know the truth of sin and how God sees both sin and sinner.

CHAPTER 5

HE SAID!

From the very beginning of man's tenure on planet Earth, the Scriptures record such statements as these,

"and he said"

"and the man said"

"and the Lord God said"

The dialogue goes on and on. God and man from the very first spoke to each other and in the perfection of the garden, there was no doubt that a harmony and directness of communication existed. After the fall, Adam and Eve no longer spoke in the openness of innocence, but addressed themselves to God with that indirect communication of guilt and blame.

Adam said as he addressed blame,

"The woman Thou gavest to be with me, she gave me…"

And then the words of Eve,

"And the woman said, "The serpent deceived me…"

It is obvious that Adam's fall changed many things; among them was man's communication with God. For it was no longer simple and direct; then complex as manifested in their changed dialogue.

We, as gospel-communicators of the glad tidings of God's amazing grace, know well the complexity of communication as it touches upon the matter of sin and condemnation. For example, "Well, I'm as good as he is," and "They are all hypocrites in the church and you really don't know what they are like," and "did you hear what the good pastor did?" and on and on goes the talk.

All at once the simple grand message of redeeming love is lost in the backwash of distorted communications that have nothing to do with the subject matter but the subject's condition. Mankind, in his fallen state, is not able to stand up to the reality of sin without immediately assessing blame to someone else's influence. They then rationalize, rectify or even deny sin and its guilt just as our original parents did.

Though all men/women are different, we are much alike in our handling of the problem of evil. Some are crude, while others are more sophisticated, intelligent and fast-tongued in relation to sin and its ensuing evil.

Whether literate or illiterate, beautiful or common, we are all "turned unto our own way."

The Apostle Paul quotes from the Psalms as he declares,

> *"Their throat is an open grave, with their tongues they keep deceiving; the poison of asps is under their lips, whose mouth is full of cursing and bitterness."*

Notice all of the descriptions of that which has to do with speech and communication.

Jesus said it well when He spoke to the Pharisees,

> *"For the mouth speaks out of that which fills the heart."*

The very heart of mankind is "deceitful and desperately wicked." Therefore, it is no wonder that a fallen, sinful man/woman would forever assess the blame and guilt of their own heart to someone else with such terms as, "They said," "They did it!" or in that often used adage when avoiding responsibility, "The devil made me do it."

It is inborn, even in the heart of a child, to assess blame for even the most childish mistake or failure with such phrases as "He/she made me do it." We always have a tough time with, "You are absolutely right, I am at fault."

Fallen mankind is completely cut off from God-life in their spiritual blindness and are incapable of seeing how guilty and sinful they are. At their very best, they can admit human error, but never do they see themselves as criminal and guilty before God's love and grace with "no standing."

On a scale of one to ten, mankind may give themselves a high score; but in our standing before God, "we all are sinners" and "none do good." We must never make our human measurements, God's measure. Before Him who knows and searches the heart of man, we are all "undone" and there is "none good, no not one."

Human merit carries no weight before God when it comes to righteousness. It is a real possibility that a "natural man/woman" might rate high in human merit being moral, loving, warm and good natured. Yet, we must always remember God's perfect demand of absolute righteousness is based on His love and grace. We all came short of His plan and purpose for mankind. Before God we all stand condemned and guilty. The issue is never what "I say" or "he says" but what "God says."

Mankind's technology and weapons of war have changed, but mankind has never changed. Always lost and undone, seeking release from their responsibility for sin. It is only God who can bring mankind to identify their condition. Because this is so, we must be faithful to the truth of God's provision for sin as well as God's wrath against sin. Repentance means "a change of mind" and mankind must have a "change of mind" if they are to be redeemed. They are turned by the drawing power of God from their self-righteousness to the righteousness of God in Christ. Mankind in and of themselves cannot make this happen.

John declared the words of Christ when he said,

> *"It is the Spirit who gives life; the flesh profits nothing; the words that I have spoken to you are spirit and life."*

Simon Peter said of Christ,

> *"He alone has the words of life."*

We must, as witnessing **AMBASSADORS** know God's Word and be indwelled with its truth. The natural person busies themselves with the authorities of men, society and religion. Thus we do not counter them by debate and well-turned phrases. Rather we must declare the truth of the "Word of God," simply and clearly.

Scripture declares,

> *"...no other Word given among men whereby a man can be saved."*

John Miller writes,

> *"What we seek, in short, is to get enough truth before men in a personal, loving manner that they may see their responsibility to act before the hour of opportunity has passed. A witness empowered by Biblical boldness is clear, compassionate, confrontational and confident; confident that the Holy Spirit who inspired the testimony will also apply it to the hearts of those who hear."*

Our power as a witness is not "they said," "he said," or "I said," but "God said". Mankind by nature in his fallen state forever clings to many authorities and philosophies that he holds equal to the Scriptures. The Bible to him is just a good book of highly inspired literature on the same level as any other great literature.

Mankind in general views the Bible as a compilation of books by human authors who by their sincere effort gives moral instruction. The idea that God has spoken anything is foreign to their thinking. The Bible, in the light of human thought is the word of man, about a god of some kind, somewhere, and carries no supernatural authority. Thus, "God says" is equal to "he, they, we or I said."

Adam gave Eve equal standing with God when he declared the woman that He had given him had imparted to him that which was forbidden. In his disobedience, he willfully took of it, making her offer equal to the command of God. Eve put the serpent's verbal gymnastics on an equal with God's command; and in so doing plunged the whole of created order into condemnation and chaos. The Apostle Paul dealt with the Judaizers who misrepresented the Gospel in relation to the law and grace and he called their communication an "accursed gospel." Mankind has no permission to tamper with the truth of God, misrepresent it or change it. The truth of God is of no "personal interpretation."

The Apostle Peter wrote,

> *"For no prophecy was ever made by an act of human will, but men were moved by the Holy Spirit spoken from God."*

We who would be faithful witnesses must live the life and walk the talk.

Brother James wrote,

> *'But prove yourselves doers of the Word, and not merely hearers who delude themselves."*

"Let your light so shine before men that they might see your good works and glorify your Father which is in heaven."

The Apostle Paul wrote,

"Be careful to maintain good works for these are good and profitable unto men."

It is the Spirit God in a believer that sets his speaking of the Scripture apart from all other authorities that men cling to. God has ordained that His Word and His life must indwell us so that mankind will hear what the believer lives.

A.W. Tozer said it this way,

"Theological facts are like the altar of Elijah on Carmel before the fire came, correct, properly laid out, but altogether cold. When the heart makes the ultimate surrender, the fire falls and true facts are transmuted into spiritual truth that transforms, enlightens, sanctifies. The church or the individual that is Bible taught without being Spirit taught (and there are many of them) has simply failed to see that truth lies deeper than the theological statement of it. Truth cannot aid us until we become participators in it."

I recall a statement somewhere from my past that was credited to Dr. Harry Ironsides. He said concerning man's failure to speak with love, that such a man could be as "clear as glass but as cold as ice."

People all around us are daily delivering many ideas about God and religion. They will accept human history as true, but they will not believe the truth of God. It is absolutely evident that God must speak to the life of mankind if he is to believe and know Him.

We are reminded by the disciple John,

> "If we receive the witness of men, the witness of God is greater; for the witness of God is this, that He has borne witness concerning His Son. The one who believes in the Son of God has the witness in himself."

The Apostle Paul declared,

> "Let your speech always be with grace, as it were with salt, so that you may know how you should respond to each person."

CHAPTER 6

THE KING IS COMING

Genesis chapter three reveals the Lord God as the first evangelist. It is through His redemptive activity that we as believer-witnesses view the grand picture of God's redeeming love and grace as well as His absolute justice and judgement. Since the days of the Old Testament, "the King is coming" has been on the lips of the prophets. By this reference attention has been called to the coming of our Lord Jesus Christ.

We contemporary believers also declare that the King has come, often to the dismay of those unbelievers around us who know nothing of His coming into this woefully frustrated world. It is my honest belief that we, as believers, must awaken to our overwhelming responsibility to declare to the world of our day the triumphant fact that indeed "the King has come."

He appeared a second time for salvation as the "Lamb of God" in payment of the sins of the world. We modern believers with our daily pressures and problems appear to have become overly preoccupied with looking up because our "redemption draweth nigh" and have overlooked the fields "white unto harvest" and not realized that our redemption has already come.

The promise of the evangel of Genesis was that,

> *"The seed of woman would come and bruise the head of the serpent while the serpent would bruise his heel."*

That was the first proclamation of the Gospel, a triumph and hope in a world depressed by the sin of its first citizens. The message of hope that we herald today to lost mankind is not "the King is coming," but we declare instead, "the Messiah our King has come;" and with His coming came both grace and truth.

We are commissioned to make disciples of all nations. Yet we know that this does not mean to convert the whole world, but to evangelize and disciple all nations. The message of grace declares the "good news" that the "Redeemer has come" in fulfillment of the promise made to Adam and Eve in the garden.

We can, with great joy and assurance, proclaim with John the Baptist,

> *"Behold the Lamb of God that taketh away the sins of the world."*

The Messiah has come and we must be busy about our arduous and joyous task of discipling all nations. Our primary commission and responsibility is to declare faithfully, daily, consistently and tenaciously,

"Look to the Lamb of God and be saved" for He has come to *"seek and to save that which is lost."*

Christ's coming in 70AD – fulfilling Matthew 24 – in judgment as promised, empowers believers to comfort one another with the knowledge that His promise was kept.

In the intimacy of the hearts of all believers and in our gatherings for ministry and instruction we should declare first and foremost the coming of the Saviour. We need to proclaim His virgin birth, His sinless life, His death, burial and resurrection according to the Scriptures and His promised coming in judgment of Israel which He did indeed accomplish.

We must declare victoriously that Jesus Christ is the power of God unto salvation and His coming was a grand promise of hope, first given to Adam and Eve in the garden. That was the first promise of the Messiah's coming. The truth of His coming in judgement to confront Israel's unbelief is for the comfort of all believers and is a noble truth declaring His promise as fulfilled. The error of end-time myths and absurdities has sparked the imaginations of believers and unbelievers filling the coffers of those who titillate and play in the grandstands in the name of last day speculations.

The proclaiming of the Gospel and discipleship is our divine commission and as believer-witnesses we must hold to our victorious mission and message at all cost, declaring it as our primary mission.

Concerning this good news, Michael Green writes,

> *"Christianity burst on the world with all suddenness of good news: good news proclaimed with great enthusiasm and courage by its advocates, and backed up by their own witness and experience. It was the fruit of their conviction that God had transformed and apparent defeat of Good Friday into the supreme victory of Easter Day."*

We too must be given to the joyful spontaneity of the Gospel. Perhaps we have grown to be form oriented and too locked into rituals and programs with too much sophistication in performability and encumbered with dead, fatigued methods. These forms do not spring from the Scriptures, but are boring hangovers from a past glory. Our ministries should minister the Word from the heart, set on fire by the HOLY SPIRIT.

Michael Green again observes,

"Christianity is enshrined in the life; but it is proclaimed by the lips. If there is a failure in either respect, the Gospel cannot be communicated."

The message of the Gospel is the supreme message for our world. If we are to disciple all nations this Gospel must be preached. Much damage has been done by overly zealous believers, who instead of directing their zeal to the evangelizing of the lost and the redemptive implications of the first coming, have created terrible distractions for the natural man in drawing him away after fancy and speculation that appeal to his curiosity.

We are the church victorious in a **HURTING** world, victimized by religions of many kinds. The discipling of new believers has not been taken seriously enough. Birthing a child is one thing, but raising the child to maturity is another matter. Child raising is the work of discipleship and we have nurseries full of newborns who are never nurtured, taught or walked with day in and day out. This is necessary for the development of the child and the new believer.

The King has come and His people are the church. We must forever learn that we don't go to church, we are the church. We gather and scatter for encouragement and renewal,

> *"stimulating one another to love and good deeds."*

We must declare always,

> *"Christ in you the hope of glory."*

The church is not real estate and buildings, but people in whom God's grace dwells. We are temples of the Holy Spirit. It is not our job to build the church for it is God's church, bought and paid for by the blood of Jesus Christ. If we are faithful and filled with grace, He will add to the church daily such as should be saved. The King of our life is here and He alone will build his church, one believer at a time.

> *"...the LORD added to the church daily such as were being saved,"*

so declared the Scriptures.

Dietrich Bonhoeffer said it well in one of his addresses,

> *"No man builds the church but CHRIST alone. Whoever is minded to build the church is surely well on the way to destroying it; for he will build a temple to idols without wishing or knowing it. We must confess that He builds. We must proclaim He builds. We must pray to Him that He may build.*

We do not know HIS plan. We cannot see whether HE is building or pulling down. It may be the times which by human standards are times of collapse are for HIM the great times of construction. It is a great comfort which CHRIST gives to His church. He says, you confess, preach, bear witness to me; and I alone will build where it pleases ME. Do not meddle in what is MY province. Do what is given to you to do; do it well and you have done enough. But, do it well. Pay no heed to views and opinions, don't ask for judgments, don't always be calculating what will happen, don't be always on the lookout for another refuge!"

CHURCH STAY CHURCH; BUT CHURCH CONFESS, CONFESS, CONFESS, CHRIST ALONE IS YOUR LORD. FROM HIS GRACE ALONE YOU CAN LIVE. CHRIST BUILDS!

THE "KING IS COMING." THE "KING HAS COME." HE IS THE HEAD OF HIS CHURCH VICTORIOUS AND WE WHO RECEIVE THE GIFT OF HIS RIGHTEOUSNESS ARE BAPTIZED BY ONE SPIRIT INTO THE BODY OF CHRIST. WE ARE THE CHURCH, THE ISRAEL OF GOD. HE IS OUR KING, AND WE DECLARE HIS GOSPEL AND DISCIPLE HIS CHILDREN!

"Behold, what manner of love the Father hath bestowed upon us, that we should be called the sons of God: therefore the world knows us not, because it knew him not. Beloved, now are we the sons of God, and it doth

not yet appear what we shall be: but we know that, when he shall appear, we shall be like him; for we shall see him as he is. And every man that hath this hope in him purifies himself, even as he is pure." (1 John 3:1-3)

BELIEVER'S BLESSED HOPE!

CHAPTER 7

THE FRUIT OF THE WOMB

The New American Translation of the Bible declares,

> *"Without the shedding of blood there is no forgiveness of sin so Christ also, having been offered once to bear the sins of many, shall appear a second time for salvation without reference to sin."*

In Genesis three we view the first shedding of blood. God Himself slew an animal and covered Adam and Eve, trading their fig leaves (the fruit of the loom) for His provided covering (the fruit of the womb). Here, in microcosm, is the whole conflict for the first time between works and grace.

Salvation is always God's covering, never man's. Man's covering at the very best is but "filthy rags". Thus, at the fall, the entire creation was subject to "vanity" and the earth began to "wax old, as doth a garment" and ultimately "shall perish". In this fallen state and because flesh is made of the dust of the earth, it became subject to the law of decay and death. As "grass withereth....and falleth away," so shall our flesh."

In light of these truths and the fact that fallen mankind has been put under condemnation God extends His grace. As is characteristic with His nature and character, He provides a plan of redemption. Throughout history, God will again and again reveal this grace to Israel and to all mankind. The garden not only revealed God's grace in those early chapters of human history but also His wrath. HE judged mankind, the serpent and the earth with that which shall forever remind the whole universe of the fall.

After that terrible judgment, the Father immediately declared salvation's decree of blood as He covered Adam and Eve with His provision, "the fruit of the womb."

Henry Morris writes of this as follows,

> "In response to their faith, God graciously provided a covering for their nakedness. Their self-made fig leaf aprons were entirely inadequate; so God made coats of skin and clothed them (Genesis 3:21). They learned, in type, that an atonement (or covering) could only be provided by God and through the shedding of blood on the altar (Note Leviticus 17:11). We do not know, of course, but it may well be that this experience also taught them that the woman's promised seed must eventually shed His own blood in the awful conflict that was coming before the full atonement could be provided. In any case, they were soon to experience

the reality of this conflict in the tragic history of their first two sons."

The very heart of the Gospel is that God has provided a sacrifice for sins, Jesus Christ, the Lamb of God, who laid down His life for the sins of the world and then was raised from the dead for our justification that we might be declared righteous. Thus, the fig leaves would never suffice for man who was condemned by the fall. He could not provide for his covering, for in his fall came his spiritual death and his utter helplessness.

The Apostle Paul declared it succinctly,

> *"...for I delivered to you as of first importance what I also received, that Christ died for our sins according to the Scriptures, and that He was buried, and that He was raised on the third day according to the Scriptures."*

Thousands of years lapsed between the garden and Golgotha, but the Lord who had promised, fulfilled His promise. That promised One was the "Lamb of God," that very one of a kind Son, by whom all things were created. He dwelt among us, bore our transgressions, and "by His stripes we are healed." Thus, all that transpired from the garden to the cross was covered by all that God instituted as a shadow of those good things to come. God gave the law to Moses, which could not justify but gave knowledge of sin. In finality, the "fruit of the womb" was that,

> "Word which became flesh and dwelt among us and we beheld His glory, the glory as of the only begotten from the Father, full of grace and truth."

> *"He came into His own and they received Him not. But as many as received Him, to them gave He the power to become the children of God, even to those who believed in His name, who were born not of the blood, nor of the will of the flesh, nor of the will of man, but of God."*

Salvation is a gift of God alone and there is absolutely no way that man contributes to its reality. It is "not of works lest any man should boast".

Our message is now and forever that God was in Christ, reconciling the world to Himself, no longer counting their sins against them, "for He has committed to us the word of reconciliation." As we faithfully give witness to these truths we can, in our mind's eye, see God in the garden as He gave the first promise of the Messiah and the first covering for sin. We must never lose God's purpose for the creation of man.

We were created to glorify Him and it is God's purpose for us that we give Him this glory by being holy and blameless. Salvation empowers man to glorify God and to enjoy Him forever. A proper theology of Biblical evangelism must always see mankind as God sees them. In so proclaiming the truth of man's condition and the reality of sin and God's provision for the penalty of sin, we provide mankind with that hearing that can produce saving faith as the Spirit of God convicts.

The Apostle Paul declared,

> "Faith cometh by hearing and hearing by the Word of God."

Charles Wesley stated this truth beautifully in the poetry of song:

> "And can it be that I should gain an interest in the Savior's blood?

> Died He for me, who caused His pain: For me, who Him to death pursued?

> He left His Father's throne above, so free, so infinite His grace!

> Emptied Himself of all but love, and bled for Adam's helpless race.

> No condemnation now I dread, I am my Lord's and He is mine;

Life in Him, my living Head, and clothed in righteousness divine.

Amazing love! How can it be, that thou my God shouldst die for me?"

In conclusion, Charles Haddon Spurgeon stated the following concerning the doctrine of atonement as it relates to the cross of our Lord Jesus Christ,

"In the cross of Christ we glory because we regard it as the matchless exhibition of the attributes of God. We see there the love of God desiring a way by which He might save mankind, aided by His wisdom so that a plan is perfected by which the deed can be done without violation of truth and justice.

In the cross we see a strange conjunction of what once appeared to be two opposite qualities—justice and mercy. We see how God is supremely just; as just as if He had no mercy and yet infinitely merciful in the gift of His Son. Mercy and justice in fact become counsel upon the same side, and irresistibly plead for the acquittal of the believing sinner.

We can never tell which of the attributes of God shines most glorious in the sacrifice of Christ; they each one find a glorious high throne in the person and work of the Lamb of God that taketh away the sin of the world. Since it has become, as it were, the disc which reflects the character and perfections of God, it is meant that we should glory in the Cross of Christ and none shall stay us of our boasting."

We, as believer-witnesses should proclaim clearly both the promise and the fulfillment of the "Fruit of the Womb." This is the work of an **AMBASSADOR** daily.

Part 2

THE TRUTH

WHAT IS TRUTH? IT ECHOES OUT OF HISTORY'S PAST UNTIL THIS VERY DAY. MANKIND HAS BEEN GLAD TO ACCOMMODATE THE QUESTION TIME AND AGAIN. SOME MAN, WOMAN OR GROUP HAS BEEN WILLING TO DEFINE TRUTH FOR THE REST OF US TIME AND AGAIN. THUS, WE HAVE OFTEN BEEN FOOLED, CONNED, DEFINED AND CONDEMNED TO FUTILITY. THE BOTTOM LINE IS THAT TRUTH LEADS TO TRUE FREEDOM. MANKIND HAS BEEN TOO OFTEN DECEIVED WITH DARKNESS AS LIGHT AND GREATER BONDAGE THE RESULT. JESUS DECLARED, "YOU SHALL KNOW THE TRUTH AND THE TRUTH SHALL MAKE YOU FREE"! HE IS TRUTH AND HE IS FREEDOM FROM RELIGION, SIN AND SELF! (JOHN 8:32) THESE CHAPTERS WILL REVIEW SOME OF THOSE AGENDAS.

CHAPTER 8

WHERE IS THE WATER?

At the well of Sychar Jesus asked for a drink of water from a Samaritan woman. She became so curious at such an unusual occurrence that she sought information concerning the "living water" spoken of as their conversation progressed.

That strange prophet from Nazareth had said to her,

> *"If you know the gift of God, and who it is who says to you, 'Give me a drink,' you would have asked Him and He would have given you living water."*

The very words "living water" strikes a responsive chord in all of us, for each of us has known thirst. Water is the most marvelous of creations to which all men are forever drawn. This marvelous encounter between Christ and the woman at the well no doubt reflects that eternal quest of man for water "by which he pitches his tents," raises his crops, satisfies his thirst and takes his pleasure from her beauty and her deeps.

Man always casts his lot where there is water. All good water is "living water." That day, at the well of

Sychar in the heat and dust of the day the Samaritan woman encountered a different kind of water. In drinking it she would never thirst again.

In her understanding she perceived a prophet, perhaps that Messiah who was to come, for had He not told her everything she ever did? "Is this not the Christ?" She knew the question, she received the answer, she drank deeply of that "living water."

It was the righteous man of Scripture about whom it is spoken as being "firmly planted by streams of water." It was John who quoted Jesus as,

> "He who believes in Me, as the Scriptures said, "From his innermost being shall flow rivers of living water."

The use of the term "living water" always reminds me of my many visits to the mountains and the artesian springs that unceasingly flow forth cool and pure.

The Gospel of Christ is the "Good News" of our Lord Jesus Christ springing forth as that living water. He became flesh and is revealed by that written word that we might know that we have eternal life. Only when men tamper with, hustle or peddle the truth does it become unclear and polluted. Thus, when made impure by error, Paul declared it as "another gospel" or an "accursed message."

The communication of that greatest of all messages, "the Good News of Jesus Christ," is the greatest privilege and highest mission that one can ever know. Yet, as with every genuine article, there is always the counterfeit or the facsimile. Whether it is those who sensationalize the truth, peddle and hustle the truth, or distort and confuse the truth, they are all distorters of the truth and therefore polluters of the "living water."

These next few chapters deal with those false ideas and notions that bubble forth from wells that are empty of clear, clean water. Those empty holes are many and often involve millions of dollars. There are many thirsty souls who drink daily from these empty wells, hoping to quench their thirst. An empty or polluted well can never satisfy one's thirst for truth. A well that is full of pollution is just as empty to a thirsty man as a dry hole. It is useless when he is seeking a cool drink of pure water.

Paul called the message that would turn men from the truth a "myth." Isn't it strange that those who do damage to the integrity of God's Word speak of the Holy Writ as being filled with "myth?" The empty wells of theology that deny the Word of God are in evidence everywhere today. Even some Bible-believing schools now deny the authority of Scripture and make fun of those who believe in the absolute infallibility and authority of Scripture. The empty wells of modern and not so modern theology have been polluted by man's unbelief.

Francis Schaeffer writes,

> *"What does God say to our generation? Exactly the same thing that He said to Israel 2,500 years ago when He said through Ezekiel, 'I am broken with their whorish heart which hath departed from me and with their eyes which go a whoring after their idols.' I believe that this is how God looks at much of the modern church and at our Western culture. I believe that this is how He looks at much of our cinemas, much of our drama, much of our art and above everything else this is the way He looks at the churches in which the gospel that is not gospel is being preached. God is saddened. Should we not be moved"?*

These empty wells are numerous today and it is next to impossible to deal with them all. Mankind daily devises some new twist or distortion of the truth. Even orthodoxy without orthopraxy becomes a perversion of the truth. James reminds us that we are not only to believe right, but we are commanded to live righteously in Christ Jesus.

Legalism with its absolute law of truth without the Spirit of that truth is deadly in its error and outcome.

The saddest matter of all is that impure or distorted truth does not die with its founder, but lives on to curse further generations.

We should also note that over emphasis, as well as under emphasis of any given truth creates error. We must determine to faithfully search the Scriptures and "rightly divide the Word of truth" that we might "know the truth."

Jesus said,

> *"Ye shall know the truth and the truth shall set you free."*

Thus, a theology that is drawn from "empty wells" of mankind's bankrupt mind and nature has often brought upon the church "spiritual apostasy."

Addressing this problem, Francis Schaeffer wrote,

> *"What is apostasy? It is spiritual adultery. No other words will do. This must be taken into account as we speak of the practice of the purity of the visible church. Do not be only academic when you speak concerning the new Molech. Nobody escapes, even if he has been raised in a Christian home and has been a Christian from the time he was young. What God wants from us is not only doctrinal faithfulness but our love day by day, not in theory mind you, but in practice. Those of us who are children of God must realize the seriousness of any part of it. But at the same time, we must be the loving,*

true bride of the divine bridegroom in reality and in practice, day by day, in the midst of the spiritual adulterer of our day. The call is not only to be the bride faithful, but also the bride in love."

As we view briefly some empty wells of both belief and practice, may we allow the Word of God to be our absolute standard.

Howard Lindsell says,

> *"Evangelicals today need to return to a view of Scripture that regards it as historical and they need to be willing to believe what it says. The implications are clear. The Bible is taken at its face value and the claims of Scripture as to its own inspiration and inerrancy are the basis on which this approach is made."*

By believing and knowing God's Word we are enabled to discern those who pollute the Word as well as those who hustle its truth for "ill-gotten gain" or "self-glory."

The Apostle Paul said it well to the Ephesians,

> *"I know after my departure savage wolves will come in among you, not sparing the flock; and from among yourselves men will arise speaking perverse things to draw away the disciples after them."*

Paul spoke of those who peddle and hustle the Word deceptively. The enemies of the truth are many and we must be on guard, not only for those who would pollute the water of life, but those "unholy dippers" who would serve the Word in a corruptible manner for money.

Finally, Paul the Apostle has warned us as believers, to become stabilized in our faith, not being carried away "to and fro" by every wind of doctrine or false teaching that leads to apostasy. Therefore, we must watch for those whose activities are described in the Greek New Testament as being "cleverness unto the craftiness of error." Craftiness or wiles in the Greek New Testament is "methodeia" from which we get the word "method."

The Theological Dictionary of the New Testament says concerning "methodeia",

> "In the N.T. 'methodeia' occurs only in Ephesians. Eph. 4:14 warns against the activities of men who have not attained to assurance of faith. In 6:11 the readers are summoned to 'put on the whole armor of God that you may be able to stand against the wiles of the devil.' They are distinguished not so much by technique or strategy as by refinement and insidiousness. (Vulgate "cunning attacks"; a.V."Wiles") If this be so however, methodeia is also used in a bad sense in 4:14. What is

meant is not 'methodical confusion of the truth,' but a cunning process which seeks to deliver up to error, or such as is proper to error. In the post-apostolic fathers only 'methodeuo' occurs, the sense being 'to distort'."

Today, in the contemporary church, we speak of methods with very little thought to the root of the word. It appears that we have, in our unbelief, not been able to trust God's sovereignty to produce the Godly results that are promised by His Word. Therefore, we reach into our bag of methods and seek to accomplish by the strength of the flesh that which God alone can accomplish by His Word and His Spirit.

It is no wonder that there has been so much distortion of truth and often no proper harvest. In haste for the harvest that is called the results, believers often act on the impulses of the flesh rather than wait on the harvest in God's time. Harvest time is a true result of faithful sowing and reaping whether the results are immediate or delayed. "Methodeia" produces a mere caricature of "true evangelism."

This is an indictment of our lack of faith and our failure to "pray the Lord of the harvest" that He might send His laborers into the harvest and give the increase in His own way and in His own time.

Scripture declares that,

> "...the Lord added to their number daily those who were being saved as they manifest grace before all the people."

Often the Scriptures refer to divine truth as water. It is essential to be faithful to this water of life that flows from the Father alone.

Dr. Harry Rimmer has written concerning the preciousness of water,

> "Highly significant is the magnificent figure of speech the Lord used when He used water to symbolize eternal life. Water is indeed the fit symbol of life, as every drop teems with it. Whether it be the salt water of the boundless sea, the alkaline pool in the desert waste, the sweet waters of the babbling brook or the moisture that is in the plants and the trees; every drop of water is a little world that teems with life."

Not only does water contain life; it also prolongs and extends it. Water saves life as many can testify who all but perished on the desert sands and were restored to life by a few drops of water. Many a lost creature who failed to find water in time, if they could speak would say that water saves and conserves life.

So, it is significant that Jesus should say to the woman of Samaria as they conversed by the well,

"Whosoever shall drink of the water that I shall give him shall be in him as a well of water, springing up into everlasting life."

We need to always be faithful to that eternal "living water." We must never muddy it with pretense and arrogance turning the truth of God into a lie. Rather, we must let the God of all righteousness be found true and every man a liar. Only from those who were made righteous by Jesus Christ shall flow "rivers of living waters." Let us therefore proclaim the truth that to know is to be set free. Have a drink!

"Let the Spirit and the Bride say, 'Come'. And let the one who is THIRSTY come; let the one who wishes take the WATER OF LIFE without cost."

CHAPTER 9

ALL NATURAL

It is with great regularity these days that I see labels that read "all natural ingredients." In this plastic, cosmetic society it appears that man needs to solve his many problems of health and body by a return to the "all natural." This represents a return to the basics. Humankind has wearied of too many synthetics, from food to fibers. The consumer has rebelled and the marketplace has adjusted. This, though good for the body, is not necessarily good for the believer.

In the realm of the spiritual, it is the "supernatural" not the natural that should take the day. Yet, in this spiritual dimension of the believer's life, many have returned again and again to that soulish, emotional experience as their rule of life. We have allowed our spiritual lives to be affected by the "it feels good" philosophy rather than the disciplines that exhilarate, but demand much more time and effort opening our understanding.

The line of least resistance has always appealed to man in his "natural state." It is no wonder then that the carnal believer returns to this weakness of the flesh and becomes a victim rather than the victor.

The Apostle Paul spoke of man in the natural when he said,

> *"The natural man does not understand the things of God, nor can he for they are foolishness to him because they are spiritually discerned."*

Scripture demands that we,

> *"Study to show ourselves approved unto God, workmen that needs not to be ashamed rightly dividing the Word of Truth."*

We, as believers, also have this tendency to follow the line of "least resistance." As a result, we have often chosen to use man's methods to do God's work. We have far too often proved ourselves successful, but much the poorer in that our results are anything but enduring and eternal.

The modern church thus finds itself the inheritor of great numbers of humanity with some kind of "religious experience," but apparently with no new direction or nature to bear it out. The natural wisdom of the flesh touched only by "God talk" and surface exposure to spiritual truths leaves the life unchanged.

The word "repentance" in the N.T. is "metanoeo" in the Greek N.T and means a change of mind.

If I were traveling in a certain direction and was warned of impending doom that lay ahead in that direction, I most certainly would change my mind about proceeding further. With that change in mind would come a change of direction to avoid calamity. In repentance, a change of mind involves a change of direction that is brought about by God's great love wherein He loved me.

Paul the Apostle made this clear to Titus,

> *"For we also once were foolish ourselves, disobedient, deceivers, enslaved to various lusts and pleasures, spending our life in malice and envy, hateful, hating one another. But when the kindness of God our Savior and His love for mankind appeared, He saved us, not on the basis of deeds which we have done in righteousness, but according to His mercy, by the washing of regeneration and renewing by the Holy Spirit, whom He poured out upon us richly through Jesus Christ our Savior, that being justified by His grace, we might be made heirs according to the hope of eternal life."*

The ingredients of this truth are from God and there is neither mixture of metaphors nor any confusion concerning who we were and how we now stand by His "amazing grace." It is only when man persists in bringing those natural and human ingredients in the form of rationalism and self-righteousness that he stumbles. We can never rely upon the "all natural" ingredients of human wisdom.

Billy Graham declared in his book WORLD AFLAME (Crusade Edition) the following,

> "Multitudes of Christians within the church are moving toward the point where they reject the institution that we call the church. They are beginning to turn to more simplified forms of worship. They are hungry for a personal and vital experience with JESUS CHRIST".

James gives a vivid description of that cake of life that is cooked up with ingredients of natural wisdom when he says,

> *"This wisdom…is earthly, natural, demonic…If you have bitter jealousy and selfish ambition in your heart, do not be arrogant and so lie against the truth. For where jealousy and selfish ambition exist, there is disorder and every evil thing."*

The day of "all natural" religion is upon us. It uses a spiritual vocabulary, the Bible, and is always given to believing "every word in the Bible including the cover." Yet, often its lifestyle and high material living leave in their wake much confusion. It speaks of material success as if it were one of the nine fruits of the Spirit.

What is being done is what Paul absolutely refused to do and that is to "peddle or hustle the Word of God." In a later chapter we will speak more pointedly to this perversion of truth.

It appears that once one lets the bars down at any point in these matters it is not long before the whole gate is down and often we fail to realize the hideousness of the situation. There is a tendency these days not to speak out for fear of appearing out of harmony with "last days world evangelism." Because of the cosmetic tendency of some forms of evangelism, there is a whole spiritual vocabulary that develops so that when spoken it figuratively rings a semantic, pietistic bell, making one a part of the "in thing."

These declare that God is absolute, perfect and able to perform what He wills. But while seeking to speak to man about God, they depend upon human attraction rather than divine intervention. In the making of disciples, these efforts are doomed for failure from their outset. Yet such activity will produce much outward movement that many in our day wrongly thrive on. Many are simply buying a well-packaged product with God's name added.

Are some truly saved amidst all this confusion and in spite of it? I would say yes, for God's Word is spoken and God honors His Word no matter how it is spoken. Even Balaam's ass was used of God to speak the truth. It is His Word and His truth that He honors and blesses. Men honor and respond to men, but God honors His Word. Thus, how we handle the Word of life and present it is of utmost importance to Biblical evangelism.

J.J Packer says concerning our "natural methods,"

> *"Everything is accordingly planned to create an atmosphere of warmth, good humor and happiness. The meeting normally includes a good deal of music. Heavy emphasis is laid on the realities of Christian experience. The meeting leads up to an appeal for decision, followed by an after meeting or a time of personal counseling. Their breezy slickness (it is said) makes for irreverence. The attempt to give them entertainment value tends to lessen the sense of God's majesty, to banish the spirit of Worship and to cheapen men's thoughts of their Creator. The seemingly inevitable glamorizing of Christian experience in the testimonies is pastorally irresponsible and gives a falsely romanticized impression of what being a Christian is like. This, together with the tendency to indulge in long, drawn-out wheedling for decision tends to produce conversions which are simply psychological and emotional upheavals and not the fruit of the spiritual*

conviction and renewal at all. Such appeals are no more than a confidence trick. The desire to justify the meetings by reaping a crop of converts may prompt the preacher and the counselors to try and force people through the motions of decisions prematurely before they have grasped what it is really all about and converts produced in this way tend to prove at best stunted and at worst spurious and, in the event, Gospel-hardened."

Though God works through our feeble efforts, we should reject always fleshly and showy methodology. Fleshy evangelism produces questionable results. Natural theology produces denial and unbelief, so whether we are natural in what we believe or natural in what we practice, the results are similar. Therefore, an inaccurate message or an accurate message with an improper method often produces an aborted spiritual birth. In the realm of physical food, "all natural" ingredients are commendable – even desirable. When it comes to spiritual matters, we had best accept only that marked "all supernatural," believing God for the increase.

CHAPTER 10

GOD TOLD ME!?

Jeremiah declared,

> *"Thus says the Lord of hosts, 'Do not listen to the words of the prophets who are prophesying to you. They are leading you into futility; they speak a vision of their own imagination, not from the mouth of the Lord."*

Ezekiel proclaimed concerning the same problem when he said,

> *"Then the Word of the Lord came to me saying, "Son of man, prophesy against the prophets of Israel who prophesy from their own inspiration. Listen to the Word of the Lord!" Thus says the Lord God, "Woe to the foolish prophets who are following their own spirit and have seen nothing."*

History is replete with illustrations of men who have spoken in the name of Almighty God. In so doing they have set both the fate of individuals and nations. The masses are forever looking for someone to call the plays and meet their needs. The magic phrase is always "God told me!" There are conniving, unscrupulous men who are always waiting in the wings of history to be that "messiah." When will we ever learn? It was Winston Churchill who gave us the insight,

> "One thing we learn from history is that we do not learn from history."

History moves forward, revealing the "comings and goings" of many varied and different spokesmen. This is especially true in the arena of religion. There is never a dearth of men and women who will take upon themselves to be the "newly sent" redeemers of mankind. They supposedly receive the latest word from the Almighty by which we all can supposedly prepare for the end of the world or that soon to be revealed Utopia.

At such junctures in history man encounters those twins of deception known as comedy and tragedy. We often laugh to keep from crying at the vulnerability of man in relation to the use of God's name in conjunction with some new-found revelation. This is not new in man's experience, for thousands of years ago Jeremiah and Ezekiel had dealings with God concerning such deception.

From what we know of man, we must assume that he is incurably religious. On the basis of this presupposition, man, in his fallen state, continually clothes himself with the "fruit of the loom." That becomes his patched together theology or philosophy by which he seeks to save himself and mankind.

Francis Schaeffer said it well when he wrote,

> *"People have presuppositions and they will live more consistently on the basis of these presuppositions than even they themselves may realize. By 'presuppositions' we mean the basic way an individual looks at life, his basic world view, the grid through which he sees the world. People's presuppositions are grids for all that they believe about life and their world. Their presuppositions also provide the basis for their values and thus their decisions."*

Within all men there is a sense of God carried over from man's initial relationship with God in the garden. It is alluded to in Romans as the witness of conscience within man and the witness of creation about man. This being the case, man is ever seeking someone or something to fill the vacuum or void in his life. And if this is so, it explains why mankind has taken to themselves many strange and devious bedfellows. These bedfellows extract devotion, power and wealth from them like a blood leach that sucks them dry. Not only men, but also nations, have been duped in the same way by the evil "messiahs." Such persons declare that they have come to deliver mankind and without a blush proclaim, "The will of God."

Virginia Mollenkott has written,

> *"I have in my short life observed only too many people who were demagogues within their own sphere of influence, burning with a 'moral' zeal, absolutely assured that their will and the will of God was synonymous.   If anyone criticized them, he was obviously of the Devil. Any attack was a satanic attack. These people were totally off balance because it never occurred to them to question the rightness of their own thinking. They bulldozed other people in the name of Christ and apparently fell asleep without a minute's soul-searching.   Within all religions, I suppose their name is Legion."*

Hardly a day goes by that we don't read or hear someone who in God's name has given the final word of revelation for the souls on the Ark of planet Earth. There have been many men in human history who have assumed the position of being one of the minds of God.

Adolf Hitler is one outstanding example as is attested to by the following dictation approved by Hitler's Ministry of Enlightenment and Propaganda,

> *"Jesus and Hitler. As Jesus freed men, Hitler freed German people from destruction.   Jesus and Hitler*

persecuted, but while Jesus was crucified, Hitler was raised to be Chancellorship…Jesus strove for Heaven, Hitler for win and Hell, so German Earth."

It is evident that Hitler saw himself as a Messiah with a divine mission to save Germany and on occasion during the 1920's he declared,

"In driving out the Jews, I remind myself of Jesus in the Temple."

At another time he said,

"Just like Christ, I have a duty to my own people."

Finally, at a Christmas celebration in 1926, Hitler, who was evil incarnate, compared his own historical importance with that of Jesus, declaring that he would be starting a new age in the history of the world. Hitler said,

"What Christ began…he [Hitler] would complete."

In a speech on February 10, 1933, he paraphrased the Lord's Prayer promising that under him a new kingdom would come on Earth, and his would be the power and the glory, Amen, and if he did not fulfill his mission, that he could be crucified.

To us who lived through the hell of World War II, we wince to think that a mere man would say such bold and wicked things using the name of our Lord Jesus Christ with which to identify his causes. Yet, it is not rare for men to do this daily in one way or another.

We believers can also fall into the trap of seeing ourselves called in some unique and extra-biblical way to speak in God's name. As New Testament believers, we must forever guard the teaching of the "priesthood of the believer." The immature and the fleshy believers are especially susceptible to error.

Paul the Apostle said,

> "There is one mediator between God and man, the man Christ Jesus."

We must resist any usurpation of God's authority and regard it as insensitivity to divine truth that produces a "God complex." We all have known this experience at one time or another. It manifests itself with a heavy emphasis on judgment of another. It is called "playing God" in another's life. We, as witnesses to God's "good news" must be very sensitive to both God and man, being very careful that we speak what God said accurately, but also lovingly.

Of more recent vintage, this terrible truth has been brought to our attention by the likes of Jim Jones of the Guyana Massacre.

Charles Krause said the following of Jones,

> *"The Reverend Jim Jones in the final days at his People's Temple colony in the Guyana jungle was the paranoid messiah of a terrorized but devoted congregation. He professed at times to be the spiritual heir of Christ and/or Lenin. He spouted a doctrine of apostolic socialism while appropriating to the Temple's treasury millions of dollars worth of property, cash and the Social Security and welfare checks of his flock."*

Here again is a record of sick religion and mixed-up utopia politics promising what no man could ever deliver. Jones quoted Scripture and insisted on being called "Father," a title of self-imposed goodness that was blasphemous. With all the hype of this man's life went the pitiful promises by way of publicity and advertisement.

Claimed for this demigod was the following,

> *"Pastor Jim Jones …Incredible …Miraculous …Amazing …The most unique prophetic healing service you've ever witnessed! Behold the Word made incarnate in your midst! God works as timorous masses are passed in every service. Before your eyes, the crippled walk and the blind see! Details of lives that only God could reveal! Christ is made real through the most precise revelations and the miraculous things in this ministry of His servant. Jim Jones."*

When will mankind learn that there is absolutely no mediator between God and man except the man "Jesus Christ"? No man but the living Christ is the vicar of another's soul. Again, in both of these illustrations we had natural men posing as gods and followers who are not "true believers;" or, if they are, they are at best "newborn" without understanding and surely are "dull of hearing."

This indeed is a great tragedy, but even greater is the "messianic" mentality that creeps in and is often found among Christian workers. Therefore, any man who has a hearing can corrupt and become a "tin messiah" to the many or few who will hear, follow and support his personal interpretation of man, God and history in the light of his own failing presuppositions.

There are many false shepherds who speak freely of God, but have no clear understanding of salvation or Bible truths. They control the minds of their hearers with "God talk" that is distorted and self-serving. Much of their theology can be summarized in, "If you want it, you can get it and if you see it, you can have it"!

Again and again, man is victimized by his own utopian idealism and presuppositions about God. Without the Word of God and the enlightenment of the Spirit by which salvation comes, man cannot know God. Mankind, in the natural, without divine revelation and supernatural truth, finds only human emptiness and a perverted understanding of God.

My library is filled with books that purport to speak for God. They speak of many esoteric conclusions about God and His Word, promising me success, healing, money, power and wealth if I will but buy their books, subscribe to their formulas and support their revelations. I am ill with it all!

God's Word declares loud and clear,

> *"But know this first of all, that no prophecy of Scripture is a matter of one's own interpretation, for no prophecy was ever made by an act of human will, but men moved on by the Holy Spirit spoken from God."*

We must "search the Scripture" and "study…to rightly divide the Word of truth." If not, we will be left to those "savage wolves" that will deceive us or find our lives misguided by those who "will arise among our own selves." Let us each one as believers "be on guard," knowing the will of God for us while faithfully functioning within the cherished positions of the "priesthood of the believer."

Donald Day Williams writes,

> *"Therefore, our reasoning within the life of faith ought to be free from the lifeless abstractions and mistaken pretensions of faithless reason. We should never suppose to possess as his own, a knowledge which only God can give. God's Word judges all human words. This brings to mind Luther's triumphant declaration, 'This is the golden age of theology. It cannot rise higher; because we have come so far as to sit in judgment on all the doctors of the church and test them by the judgment of the apostles and prophets'."*

Men and their teachings must always stand in judgment by God's Word with studied consideration. The teachings of men produce fruits that evidence of what sort they are. God has given us His Truth and His Spirit by which we are taught that Truth. Truth always demands responsibility, and it is shown in our lives by our obedience to Christ. This same Truth also demands that we allow even our weaker brother to exercise his own priesthood as we love and encourage him.

Dietrich Bonhoeffer said it this way,

> *"Responsibility implies tension between obedience and freedom...The man of responsibility stands between obligation and freedom; he must dare to act under obligation and in freedom; yet he finds his justification*

neither in his colligation nor in his freedom, but solely in Him, who has put him in the (humanly impossible) situation and who requires this deed of him. The responsible man delivers up himself and his deed to God."

In conclusion, we realize how very complicated and complex the sinfulness of man is and how easy it is for one to say to another, "God told me" and for the other, depending on his presuppositions, to respond or resist. It is apparent that throughout history there have been those who chose to respond and fall victim to many and varied hideous distortions.

We, as contemporary believers, must resist. Our resistance demands faithfulness to both the Spirit and the Word so that we might not be motivated or manipulated into cooperation with that which is in error, whether in doctrine or method.

To become faithful witnesses, we must be knowledgeable and Spirit led in the matter of righteousness. We should be very certain when someone speaks the phrase "God told me," that we demand their source of authority. We must refuse to be led by those who speak from their own imagination or experience and not from the Word of God. We should never forget that, when men say "God said,"

Holy Words and Holy Truths should produce a real difference in our lives.

CHAPTER 11

PROPHETS OR PROFITS?

Jeremiah the prophet declared,

> *"Therefore behold I am against the prophets; declares the Lord, who steals my words from each other. 'Behold, their tongues and declare,' the Lord declares; 'Behold I am against those who have prophesied false dreams, declares the Lord, and related them, and led my people astray by their boasting, yet I did not send them or command them, nor do they furnish this people the slightest benefit; declares the Lord."*

Such days have always been with us, though never so intense and with such sophistication. Today men of numerous persuasions can readily declare to the world their brand of "God says." Because of advanced electronics and technology proclaimers can go day and night nonstop. Divine truth clearly and faithfully given will reap a grand harvest in God's time. By the same token with those who are unclear, doubt and error can spread their perversions like the plague.

Among the proclaimers, these are the days of the "big budgets" and "great profits." Therefore, the great push is on for the biggest audience possible. Because this is so, human "methodeia" has taken the day. We all have become quite jaded, skeptical and even alarmed if we have observed closely what is happening in the "religious market."

There have never been so many human prophets with the ready answer for whatever the situation, whether the proper questions have been asked or not. It seems to make little difference just so the money comes in and the bills are paid. Those bills include not just air time but whatever pet project is of concern to the speakers at that moment. When one project is complete, the vicious cycle of the "prophet and the profits" starts all over again.

The greatest commodity is always that which God can do for us so that we can be happy and successful, healthy and beautiful. Sometimes there are those more bold ministries that offer it all. Promises, promises and more promises from those who speak so beautifully about God.

The Apostle Paul said of his own speaking,

> *"And when I came to you, brethren, I did not come with superiority of speech or of wisdom, proclaiming to you the testimony of God."*

Paul would never have accepted the low standard of today's "performability" which speaks so fluently and unabashedly about the money racket. There is, of course, the promise to "PRAY for the listener" when it ought to be "PREY on the listener." Once on the mailing list, endless "mail-outs" asking for money for the present financial crisis arrive. Often the speaker writes a book especially for his video or audio audience filled with all of the promises and goodies that one could ever hope to find under one cover. To do a great work for God these days, it appears that the primary prerequisite for the successful "media ministry" or "super ministry" is not supernatural power, but natural hype. I think that Paul would have been absolutely mortified at what men have stooped to, in trying to justify their goals. This "methodeia" is sick and Paul called it "peddling the Word of God."

Again the Apostle Paul said,

> *"We have renounced the things hidden because of shame not walking in craftiness or adulterating the Word of God."*

Bob Jones Sr. once said, "One should never do wrong to do right." It is unfair to God's name and to believers to make absurd bills and take on gigantic causes and declare that "God said" to do so. Then when these same causes run into difficulty or trouble, these same self-appointed prophets turn to the public at large and declare that God told them to do it; and you are to pay for it! What absurdity! Local churches and fellowships, whether large or small, should be careful, waiting on the Lord, and not overextending themselves, expecting to pressure their people into paying the bills. Once this foolishness starts, all kinds of financial theories, supposedly based on the Word of God arise, most of them self-serving.

God gave us instructions in the New Testament church to,

> *"Let each one do just as he has purposed in his heart; not grudgingly or under compulsion; for God loves a cheerful giver."*

In our do-it-yourself mentality, we have often taken the work of God into our own impatient hands and set out to work for God, before God has done a work in us. God will never fail in that which is of Himself. It is never wrong to quietly make a need known to other believers. To create great indebtedness and then declare our financial accountability before the world, begging people to join in our financial gymnastics, borders on the obscene.

Another source of frustration is the "spiritual name clubs" that are joined, depending on the amount given. The religious books, records, artifacts from the Holy Land and other holy "junk" that are given away for the bucks received is absolutely ludicrous. We must never forget all of this unholy commotion is being viewed by the world. I am sure they wonder, as do we, where it will all end. Though many ministries are faithful and discreet, it is the noisy, pushy proclaimers who confuse the world. Some speak of heaven and eternal life while expanding their financial holdings and real estate below. There possibly is certainly a good reason to have and maintain buildings for ministry as well as monies for air time. Yet, they must be under God's control that we might have a proper testimony.

The Apostle Paul said it well,

> *"I have coveted no one's silver or gold or clothes. You yourselves know that these hands ministered to my own needs and to the men who were with me. In everything I showed you that by working hard in this you must help the weak and remember the words of the Lord Jesus that Himself said, "It is more blessed to give than to receive."*

Paul also gave us some idea of a proper procedure in collecting our monies for the work of Christ as he exhorted the Corinthians to save up their generous offering over a year at home, before he came, so that people would not be affected by covetousness. He gave the proper time to do such for they had begged to participate in giving:

> "Now concerning the collection for the saints, as I directed the churches of Galatia, so do you also. On the first day of every week, let each one of you put aside and save, as he may prosper, that no collections be made when I come."

John spoke of supporting those who went out from them for the sake of the Name, accepting nothing from the gentiles. How simple it all is for God's people if they sow, water and trust God with the increase as we have been exhorted.

We have made things so tacky, complex and difficult and have made a show of that which Jesus said:

> "We should not let our left hand know what our right hand does."

In the Old Testament we are told that God's Word would not return void but would succeed in that matter for which it was sent.

In the New Testament, we are promised that,

> "God will supply all your needs according to His riches in glory in Christ Jesus."

God's work that is done God's way will produce God's results.

The whole matter of determining what is spiritually profitable from the vast field of media presentations comprises a real problem for the contemporary believer. Thus, the word "profit" takes on another meaning as we apply it to the word profitable. In our local ministries, we have a big responsibility to edify and instruct believers that they might grow into maturity and in turn minister to others. The use of televisions and radio should have specific goals and address specific audiences seeking to profit them without making profits from their generosity.

Frank Schaffer speaks to the misuse of the media, which is so prevalent today as he writes,

> *"Television itself for many reasons is a dubious enterprise. Christians and Christian imitators cannot often be told apart in this fast-growing greasy money field. They have adopted the worst of television style, studiously ignoring any creative programming and pander, as does most TV to the shallow, the frivolous, the quick fix and the sensational. {I saw one TV host claim that the satellite he was about to put up to beam his rubbish worldwide was fulfilling Biblical prophecy and was one of the angels of the last times that John saw). Most so-called Christians' efforts in television can only congratulate themselves for their massive*

fundraising efforts and subsidiary money making empires."

We must discern between what is profitable and what is for profits. This will take some maturing and growing for many of us that have far too long taken in words given with certain force and finish, as authority. We must go back to Scripture and learn what the word of man is and what the Word of God is. Only then will we be able to truly discern the prophetic from the pathetic and the prophet from the profit.

Jesus indicted the Pharisees by saying,

> *"You are mistaken, not understanding the Scriptures or the power of God."*

May we who are given the great responsibility of representing the Gospel know well the Scriptures and the power of God.

Norman Wells puts it clearly when he writes the following,

> *"We need to turn from vague vanities and listen for a victorious voice from God. We need preachers who will stand and proclaim what God has said without fear of favor. We need preachers who care not about comfortable careers but about the urgency of conveying communications from God to man. We need preachers, not pitchmen; pastors, not peddlers!"*

If we don't stand strong in this direction by divine discernment we may well become the victims like unto those so vividly described by Norman Wells in the following paragraph,

> "As glamour boy preachers who present themselves as the hero of every story they tell, and every illustration they use revealing their magnificence, they generally gather a following of what might be described as 'preacher worshippers'." They transfer the religious loyalties of the people to, promoters, evangelical executives, pulpit politicians, divine diplomats, clerical comedians, masters of ceremonies, medicine men, spiritual specialists and glamour boys. WHO NEEDS THEM"?

As informed believers, we should be "on guard" as to discerning between "prophet" and "profit." The "profit motive" can also befall the local church and often does in these highly competitive times. Here we must stand firm and guard against mixed motives and commercialization. In our churches' super structures and super budgets, there is often much waste.

Howard Snyder addresses this problem as he writes,

> "Church buildings are a witness to our pride. We insist that our church structures must be beautiful and well appointed---which usually means expensive---and justify this on grounds that God deserves the best. But such thinking may be little more than the rationalizing of

carnal pride. Or we say, perhaps, that after all we are ambassadors for the King of Kings, who is abundantly rich. True! But this does not justify spending vast resources to build embassies. We may forget that our King is at war, and we are called to be his witnessing soldiers. We have other justifications for our expensive temples. We may, for instance, feel that we must have beautiful buildings in order to draw sinners to the church and thus to Christ. But two things are wrong. The church is to seek the sinner, not visa versa. Second, the motivation is wrong. We try to attract sinners by appealing to price. This was not Christ's approach. Too often our churches end up competing with each other on the architectural plane. This is evangelism at its inflexibility, lack of fellowship, price and class divisions in the modern church."

In finality, not only the media communicators but also local fellowships and ministries of all kinds must determine the difference between the prophetic and the pathetic, the profitable and the profiting. Let us do so with eternal vigilance.

An old sage declared,

"The greatest miracle in all the world is that the Word of God has survived preachers and preaching."

BE ON GUARD!

CHAPTER 12

REVIVAL!

It was when Jacob came from Paddan-aram that God appeared a second time to him and blesses him as follows,

> "Your name is Jacob; you shall no longer be called Jacob, but Israel shall be your name. Thus, He called him Israel. God also said to him, 'I am God Almighty'; be fruitful and multiply; a nation and a company of nations shall come from you. And kings shall come forth from you, and the land which I gave to Abraham and Isaac, I will give it to you."

This promise that was given to Abraham was confirmed to Jacob and his name was changed to Israel so that all of his descendants were called Israelites. From then forward, Israel appears throughout the Old Testament as an occasional synonym for Jacob.

Israel traces its ancestry back to the twelve sons of Jacob who are referred to as the "people of Israel." There is "Israel" "the twelve tribes of Israel" and "the Israelites." Thus, Israel was to be a special covenant people by whom God would speak to all nations of

His name and by whom eventually in the "fullness of time," He would send forth His son, the Messiah.

Moses speaks of this as he declared what God had said,

> *"The Lord has today declared you to be His people, a reassured possession as He promised you, and that you should keep all His commandments; and that He shall set you high above all nations which He has made, for praise, fame and honor; and that you should be a consecrated people to the Lord your God as He has spoken. So all the peoples of the Earth shall see that you are called by the name of the Lord; and they shall fear you."*

The whole of the Old Testament is the progressive revelation of God's dealing with a prepared, called out people for a specific promised purpose. It includes their risings and fallings, their faithfulness and apostasy. The whole of the Old Testament is given to God's dealing with his particular, peculiar people. All of the prophecies, exhortations and rebukes are addressed specifically to Israel and no one else.

It is evident that the prophecies of the Old Testament were being addressed to Israel and declared God's proposed design and purpose for Israel as would be revealed in God's Messiah and the redemption of mankind as was initially promised. The promise of the old covenant becomes the fulfillment of the New Testament.

Erich Sauer declares the purpose of Israel as follows,

> "On the stage of world history by the example of Israel there should be publicly shown to the nations what sin and grace, judgment and redemption are. In Israel's paradigm, the object lesson, not to be misunderstood or ignored, such as awakens the conscience and leads the sinner to the knowledge of himself and then through repentance and faith to the knowledge of God. Theirs should be a calling which should find its final center and crown in this, that at last not only God's Word, but God Himself should come, not only His prophecy but His Son."

Thereby, Israel becomes the place of arrivals of the World-Redeemer, the bridgehead of His coming out of eternity, the home of the God-anointed (Messiah) and through Him the birthplace of the Christian Church."

> "For the spread of salvation, Israel should be God's witness and mouth, the channel of the revelation of salvation, the standard-bearer of the truth of God's herald among the nations. Herein lies the commission as prophet and missionary. The purport of its national history is associated with the universal; "in Thee shall all families of the Earth be blessed."

All Scriptures of the Old Testament are addressed and directed to Israel. None of the Old Testament Scriptures are addressed directly to the New Testament church. Paul spoke often in the New Testament about the "mystery" that was hidden from the past ages and generations. This is, of course, that revelation of Christ and His Church. Here, we, by way of the Epistles, are given explanation of that "mystery" that is now revealed.

In these days of mixed metaphor, the torn and distorted proclamation, we are often introduced to an empty well of misunderstanding in relation to the Church and Israel. This well often clouds the proper understanding of true Biblical evangelism. Many people persist in returning to the Old Testament teaching concerning revival and Israel. By the misinterpretation of the text and taking it out of context, they have developed a "revivalist theology" that is totally foreign to the New Testament revelation.

The Gospels introduce us to the first manifestation of the Church that was yet to be born at Pentecost and the climax of the old covenant that was a shadow of the good things to come. It is comprised of both Gentiles and Jews who were brought to salvation by the Gospel of Christ.

Now, in the New Testament economy, we are discipled by the dynamic and all sufficient truths of the New Testament and the Holy Spirit. Paul instructs us, as believers, how to relate to this covenant of grace, the cornerstone of redemption-history. The Epistles of the New Testament teach us how to live and reveal our origins and roots as heirs of the grace of God and joint heirs with Jesus Christ.

> *"Now these things happened as examples for us, that we should NOT CRAVE EVIL THINGS, as they also craved...do not be IDOLATERS...nor let us act IMMORALLY...nor GRUMBLE. Now these things happened to them as an example, and they were written for our INSTRUCTION."*

Thus the problem is: how can I, a child of God, sealed and indwelt with the Holy Spirit, the very temple of the Spirit, now live so that I do not fall into the trap of the aforementioned evils? The solution is not to be found in the empty well of "revivalist theology" that exhorts the believer with Old Testament passages that are related more to Israel's apostasy than to the believer's walk and America's religious pluralism. America is not Israel and cannot return to that which it never was. The Church is not Israel, and we as believers are indwelt by God Himself by His Spirit.

We no longer have the incomplete revelation of sacrifices and ceremonies, for now the shadow has surrendered to the real. For He, the Messiah, is come. The dramatic message of the seer has given way to the faithful proclamation of every believer-evangelist who is God's messenger. The gifted evangelist-specialist is not a revivalist who in the Old Testament exposed and condemned apostasy, but rather a proclaimer of the "good news" of Christ's death, burial and resurrection in payment of sin.

The New Testament nowhere reveals misuse of such terminology. Revival is a term peculiarly belonging to Israel in her apostasy and backsliding. The Church alone knows the indwelling of each believer who is individually a priest unto God. There is another difference. The priest of the Old Testament was the mediator between God and man and the prophet spoke for God to a people who had no other voice from God than his.

In the New Testament economy, we have the anointing of the Holy Spirit, who is our teacher; and we need no one to teach us. There is only "one mediator between God and man and that is the man Christ Jesus." The Holy Spirit is the called-alongside-one who guides us into all truth and teaches us all things, as He did the disciples, revealing to them the Word of God.

We also have the Father's promise to chasten those who are His; so if we grieve or quench the Holy Spirit, we will deal directly with the Father. If the New Testament is true on these points, if we are given faithful teaching-pastors to shepherd the flock and the evangelist to preach and teach salvation, there is no need of the thunderous Old Testament prophet.

The work of the New Testament evangelist is to proclaim and give witness to the good news of the Gospel that those who have never heard would be drawn by the Holy Spirit and be saved. Thus, we have often fallen prey to the misinterpretations of Scripture by those who, in their zeal to change the moral and spiritual decay of the nation, have equated America of the Church with Israel. Therefore, they have taken the stance of the Old Testament prophet and seek to exhort the nation back to God. There is no way! The Church is the Church and the principles of truth and evil as found in the Old Testament Scripture helps us see clearly the end result of fleshly behavior.

We have these so that we might be instructed as Paul said to the Romans,

"For whatever was written in earlier times was written for our instruction, that through perseverance and the encouragement of Scriptures we might have hope."

The way to fruitful, powerful and vigorous New Testament faith is knowledge and wisdom of the Word as it is both believed and lived out in our world. The answer is not to be found in preaching the salvation proclamation over and over to believers. We must give ourselves to being equipped for the work of service to the building up of the body of Christ. By such, we are enabled to "attaining unto the unity of the faith and the stature that belongs to Christ."

Thus, our growth and maturity will prevent us from being "tossed about by every wind of doctrine" and captured by the "trickery of men" or the "method" of men. Each and every believer is to do the work of service. The work of evangelism is the work of every member of the body of Christ. Each believer is to exercise the gifts of the Spirit within the body.

Secondly, it is essential to the body that those gifted in evangelism do the work of the evangelist as the New Testament presents that work, seeking to stay free of gimmicks, gadgets and other cosmetic appeals that emotionalize instead of truly evangelize. There are many false forces in evangelism and the church at every cost should stay away from them.

Lewis Sperry Chafer writes concerning this matter,

> *"In considering the true forces of evangelism as they are set forth in the Scriptures, it will be found that they, in contrast with the "false forces" already mentioned, depend upon the activity of the whole company that they demand an unceasing effort for their fullest realization; and that they, from necessity, must unusually be carried on independently of public gatherings or special leaders."*

Finally, the whole concept of revivalism as is practiced so widely in our time is neither New Testament nor Old Testament, but a concoction of immense perverted proportion. In the Old Testament revival was the putting of the Word of Yahweh into the midst of the people. Israel had listened to self-motivated and self-serving prophets who said, "Thus saith the Lord," when the Lord did not speak. Thus, she apostatized and turned from the living God to idols and pagan gods.

Manasseh, the wicked king, removed the Word and the holy things from Israel and she suffered in her sinfulness and apostasy. Then Joshua became king and restored the Word and the worship of the Almighty One among the people, bringing revival to

Israel. Revival is where the presence of God's Word is in belief and practice. Evangelism is not revivalism nor is revivalism evangelism.

There is no New Testament teaching on revival but rather a walk of faith whereby we progressively grow in grace and are renewed. We can then stand against unprincipled men and their false teachings on the outside and carnality from within. To understand the true work of the local church as the "pillar and ground" of the truth, the individual as that "royal priest" before the Lord is to properly understand that which has been provided for our spiritual growth and to "rightly divide" the Word of faith.

The absolute truth concerning revival is that it is not something you have or something you go to or something you do, but rather it is something that God gives as we are walking within that provided life of faith that His Word and Spirit provide. Thus, revival is a constant return to the basics of God's Word.

God, who said that believers are "light in the Lord," also said "walk as children of light." He has also provided all that we need to do so. The salvation of others among us is not a revival in any shape or fashion, but a harvest of evangelism.

In truth, revival is only one thing in the New Testament economy and that is stated well by John as he wrote,

> *"If we walk in the light as He is in the light, we have fellowship with one another and the blood of Jesus Christ, God's Son cleanses us from all unrighteousness."*

The empty well of misappropriated terms has caused misunderstanding that is not conclusive to sound doctrine and, therefore, not conducive to proper living. We must learn to be always faithful to the truth with which we are entrusted and not accept all that has been said about God and His Word from tradition. Then armed with these basic truths, there is never any reason that we should ever again be misled concerning this empty well. God has provided the way whereby we, the "just," can walk by faith and proceed from faith to faith.

When sin has broken fellowship with God, we must understand what God has provided for our restoration without all of the hassles of human "guilt trips" or "crisis theology." Those appeal to our emotions and immaturity rather than to God's grace. God's grace manifests itself through chastening by His Word and His Spirit through which come "restored fellowship", "a renewed life" and the "joy of our salvation."

The game of basketball in its basic rules allows a man five fouls before he is out of the game. A foul breaks the harmony of the game or the fellowship between each side and the rule book so that upon the referee's call of infraction, the guilty one must acknowledge his guilt by raising his hand thus restoring him to the game. So it is that in our daily lives, we are restored to the fellowship and the walk of faith by "confessing our sins." The impact of the word "confess" is that of "agreeing with God" that we have sinned and broken fellowship with His Spirit and His Word.

As in the game of basketball we do not have to "filibuster" with many words when we foul-sin, but rather acknowledge our transgression thereby agreeing with the "rule book" that it is right concerning what a transgression is. The referee administers the rules as the Holy Spirit administers God's Word to our lives. We must learn to confess and REBOUND!

In our transgressions as believers, it is important to confess also to the one wronged as we confess to the Father. The God of all grace, who declared us righteous by justification, continues to "child train" us when we sin so that we may confess to Him or "agree with Him" that He was right and we were wrong for we "sinned."

Even our earthly fathers forgive when we have done something wrong. We acknowledge our wrongness, agreeing with them that we were wrong; then they gladly restore us to fellowship. How much greater is God's grace and forgiveness! Let us walk in the "light" as He is in the light, daily growing in grace and truth. Then we will know that walk in the Spirit that will not "fulfill the lust of the flesh." As we know this walk, we will know the true meaning of revival, which is spiritual renewal.

Paul told Timothy where to place his emphasis,

> *"Until I come, give attention to the public reading of Scripture, to exhortation and teaching. Take pains with these things, absorbed in them, so that your progress may be evident to all. Pay close attention to yourself and to your teaching. Persevere in these things, for as you do, you will insure salvation both for yourself and for those who hear you."*

If each believer will but apply this same instruction to his own life, he will indeed experience "walking in the light" and by anybody's definition he will know the true meaning of "revival" as is revealed in the New Testament. It is this "walking in the light" that will truly renew our inner man day by day.

CHAPTER 13

THE CHARADE PARADE

According to Webster's Dictionary a charade is "a game in which a chosen word or phrase is acted out by one or more people in pantomime, syllable by syllable or as a whole so as to be guessed by those who watch."

The Lord Jesus Christ exhorted us as follows,

> *"Beware of practicing your righteousness before men to be noticed by them; otherwise you have no reward with your Father who is in Heaven."*

The three major concerns of Matthew were giving, prayer and fasting. It is these spiritual exercises that are more easily given to the dramatic. The world looks on and views these matters apart from their true meaning and without spiritual discernment. In our desire to witness, we must be cautious of things that are given to outward show. Otherwise, we cause the unbeliever-seeker problems by outward performances that are private. Jesus was concerned about the pride of man, whose tendency is to be cosmetic and superficial about religious externals.

He reminded us when we give,

> *"Do not let your left hand know what your right hand is doing that your giving of your monies may be seen in secret and your Father who sees in secret will repay you."*

The world probably misunderstands this custom or tradition more than any other and many have been turned off and driven away from the hearing of the Gospel by the brazenness and rationalization that goes along with the charade of "lifting an offering." This causes "spiritual HURT" in the unbeliever! We have often been careless with our monies, and we have confused the truth of proper New Testament financial concerns and priorities. It often appears that our right hand and our left hand have gone into business together in conspiracy to bleed the poor and the widow of their last penny to "get the Gospel out."

We have instead often left them in greater need while those who "raise their funds" with glib tongue and greedy hands have confused the issues and made of themselves "successful institutions." This is often done by distorting Scriptures and the spiritual principle concerning proper "almsgiving and alms taking. This has no doubt frustrated many who have been confused as to what the truth of God is concerning His grace and our giving.

To give is to be blessed, no doubt, and Paul said it well when he quoted Christ as saying,

"It is more blessed to give than to receive."

But Paul the Apostle sought always to be a model and an example of hard work and faithful loving and giving, by working with his own hands. He was careful about his image as a proclaimer of the Gospel though he had every right to receive money for his ministry. We must always be sensitive to unbelievers in our appeals for money. We should always seek with love and wisdom to "give as we have been blessed."

We should heed what Charles Spurgeon wrote,

"Earn all you can; save all you can; and give all you can."

In so doing we should become wise in how we give, realizing that it is commanded of us to be generous. We need to give; but in our giving we should be careful lest we fall prey to Satan's "methodeia." That is craftiness that belongs to the world system and its rulers. We must not only have right motives, but make sure our procedures for receiving and giving not become a hindrance to our witness. Thus, we conduct ourselves with wisdom toward outsiders, making the most of the opportunity.

The second great concern of our Lord was that prayer might not become that which would draw attention to the believer making praying an end in itself. This fact would cause one to take on the appearance of the Pharisee, who smote his breast while thanking God that he was better than those sinners who looked on.

The very idea of prayer as a spectacle and a charade is foreign to Scripture. The believer within the intimate confines of prayer time should be direct and specific. Public gatherings, with prayer circles, prayer lines and other such prayer spectacles before the world in public display is not only in poor taste but it is unnecessary and self-serving. Care must be taken not to become a caricature or be tacky by making the unusual or dramatic the thrust of our prayer times. We must realize that the natural man DOES NOT UNDERSTAND THE THINGS OF GOD! They are foolishness to him because he is not spiritually discerning.

Thus, we as believers, who have the opportunity to witness to unbelievers must deal with public prayer with great wisdom and discretion. We do so, not because we are ashamed of Christ but because of the personal nature of prayer. The Scriptures promise that God who hears in secret will repay us.

This is not an issue of boldness, but discretion and humility.

People often attribute piety to public praying. This is no standard at all and most often lends itself to self-righteousness. Our greatest ministry in speaking to people of God is to have first spoken to God in behalf of people. This should be done in the privacy of our own prayer life or in the intimacy of a fellowship of believers apart from the intruding eye of the world. The alternative is to create a "prayer parade" and be thought of as pious and deeply religious. God forbid! Prayer is commanded and necessary for each believer and for the body in its gatherings. We never forget the fleshiness of the old nature and how easily contrived words and pretty phrases can produce an emotional counterfeit of real prayer. We must PRAY not PREY!

True caring for others is absolutely dependent on prayer; and if we do not faithfully and persistently intercede for mankind, we shall never effectively talk to mankind about God. But prayer is never a spectacle, a show or a chance to show or manifest our piety, NEVER!

Lewis Sperry Chafer writes concerning prayer,

"How little the stupendous fact of this individual power is realized by Christians today! The present failure on the part of Christians to enter the holy place in intercession according to the appointment of God is sufficient to account for the present lack of Holy Spirit conviction and conversation in the church. Fundamentally then, the personal element in true soul-winning work is more a service work, is more a service of pleading for souls than a service of pleading with souls. It is talking with God about men from a clean heart and in the power of the Spirit, rather than talking to men about God."

Prayer is a hard and demanding work and it is not that which should put us on public display. It should be done personally and corporately in privacy and in dead earnestness away from the eye of the world. When prayer degenerates into a display and a show, it becomes a sham, inexcusable and causes hurt and misunderstanding for the unbeliever.

Jesus said,

"They that do this, already have their reward."

In conclusion, John R. Mott declares with great truthfulness,

"The missionary church is a praying church. The history of missions is a history of prayer. Everything vital to the success of the world's evangelism hinges on prayer."

Jesus said that we should "pray therefore, the Lord of the harvest that He send forth laborers into His harvest."

Fasting is the third area that Christ dealt with firmly. Because of its nature, it lends itself to the dramatic and is a feature that not only Christ attacked but also the prophets. This is a deep well that diverts from the teachings and truth of the Gospel. Fasting is important for a period of time. It diverts all of one's energies and efforts to God's Word and prayer, while little attention is given to the body and its need. Of course, one would not work or be given to physical exertion during this time by quietly and privately pulling aside from one's daily routine for a time of spiritual blessing before the Lord. This should be done without calling attention to oneself or the fact of fasting.

According to Christ, it should be done in secret and not be declared publicly, but quietly for one's own growth and communication with the Lord. The Lord who sees in secret will repay the believer for his faithfulness and devotion. Thank God that this is so! What a show it would become, a "can you top this" mentality that reveals mankind's attempt to produce outward piety by a show of the flesh.

There is not much said and written about fasting today in proper instruction for modern believers, but surely it does enhance our spiritual life, especially in a world of overabundance where we have more than we need to eat and drink. It would well behoove us to fast at times for concentration upon the things of God and intercession for world evangelism.

There are several illustrations found in the New Testament pertaining to fasting, e.g., Cornelius fasted before his vision and Paul fasted following his vision on the road to Damascus. The sending of Barnabas and Saul out on the first missionary journey was preceded by fasting. The church of the second century had days of fasting and Second Clement evaluated fasting as better than prayer.

The tragedy is that those who have "profit motives" have used this outward expression of personal faithfulness to Christ as a ploy to draw attention to this practice. At times it has become a kind of mystical "cure all" for man's spiritual ills. What a travesty!

Each of these areas that were spoken of by Christ is most important to our lives as believers and is a part of a spiritual balance that is most important to world missions.

But as has already been stated, we must be careful to be faithful in each of these things under the Spirit's promptings and not grieve the Spirit by disobedience. At the same time, we must not be drawn into a fleshly counterfeit of the real thing that has no merit or meaning and is a perversion of the truth. Wrong emphasis, as well as over-emphasis of any truth is the beginning of error that if persisted in, can create a monster of untruth or diversion from the real truth. May we be careful to never get caught up in a "charade parade" that causes great HURT to the unbeliever's ability to hear the truth of Jesus.

CHAPTER 14

WHAT WE SEE IS WHAT WE GET!

The world at large puts great stock in that which appeals to the eye and is skin deep and cosmetic. From the world has come a slogan that is spoken with tongue-in-cheek, but it is no doubt true. It is often imprinted on T-shirts and declares, "What you see is what you get."

I guess our reaction should be "let the buyer beware." Yet, in the realm of religious "methodeia" and the by-products thereof, it might be put this way, "What you see may not be what you get." Because of the fleshiness of mankind, who is often tempted to do God's work his way rather than God's way, we have produced a whole pantry full of unhealthy goodies and their miserable by-products.

It appears, as we look at the superficiality of the religious scene in America today, that we have indeed gotten what we deserve. We have courted the world's methods and now we bear her mark. A lifestyle witness is often frustrated by the many ploys and empty wells of wrong beliefs as well as practices that have often masked the true message of Jesus and the gospel.

Literally thousands of decisions are made each year and often the greater part of them are never seen or heard from after six months. The cause of such has to be the superficiality of our "methodeia" and that which it has produced, namely "decisional regeneration," which when looked at critically is not regeneration at all. Such decisions are regularly mentioned by those who are most apt at counting anything that moves in an invitation and speaking glowingly of the many making decisions. In truth, these persons may never have really understood the message or the invitation. Only a clear lifestyle presentation of the Gospel will produce the true Gospel response.

Lewis Sperry Chafer speaks forcefully to this point when he writes,

> *"A leader with a commanding personality may secure the public action of many, when the issue is made one of religious merit through some public act. Under such an impression, a serious person may stand in a meeting who has no conception of what is involved in standing by faith on the Rock, Christ Jesus. Or he may be persuaded to abandon his natural timidity, when he knows nothing of abandoning his satanic tendency to self-help, and resting by faith on that which Christ has*

done for him. If questioned carefully, the basis of assurance with all such converts will be found to be no more than a consciousness that they have acted out the program prescription for them."

This is very sad, for the Word of God makes it clear that we, as believer-witnesses we must sow and water; but it is God alone who gives the increase. We often persist in seeking to persuade men with that persuasion that is of the flesh, using the reasoning of the natural mind.

Many of the empty wells of human activity that are stated in these chapters are at this very moment in human history haunting us. As we seek to faithfully declare the Gospel to a spoiled and permissive society, we must not cater to those who view "spiritual things" on their own terms. This is well expressed in the popular song, "I Did It My Way." This has come to include, in their thinking, the precious and holy things of a sovereign God.

Salvation is the free gift of God's righteousness that is given freely to those who believe as they are drawn to the Father by His Spirit. It is not manipulated and connived into human response to satisfy the undue pressure that is put upon them by a human instrument. The conclusion of such is that they are never saved and therefore never truly discipled and cannot be. In such cases, "What we see is what we get." It is neither real nor honest, nor can it be. It is the product of man's doing.

Chafer continues to address this frustration as follows,

> "A true decision must depend upon the action of the will of the individual as he is moved by his own clear vision of his place in the saving work of Christ, and that vision must be created by the Spirit. When this is accomplished, there will be little occasion to argue and plead, and methods which are calculated to force a decision will be found to be superfluous; and any method which is superfluous is usually resented by intelligent people. Such methods create a sense of unreality, where there should be growing reality."

This is what I have chosen to call "decisional regeneration," for it is an unreal quality of life that is based upon a human decision that has simply bought an emotion time frame product that will go as it came. Its foundation is simply "human decision" and nothing else.

A.W. Tozer addresses a similar "empty well," which he calls "instant Christianity," and he writes as follows,

> "It is hardly a matter of wonder that the country that gave the world instant tea and instant coffee should be

the one to give it instant Christianity. The American genius for getting things done quickly and easily with little concern for quality or permanence has bred a virus that has infected the whole evangelical church in the United States and, through our literature, our evangelists and our missionaries, has spread all over the world. By 'instant Christianity,' I mean the kind found almost everywhere in gospel circles and which is born of the notion that we may discharge our total obligation to our own and we are permitted to infer from this that there is no reason to seek to be saints by character. An automatic, once-for-all quality is present here that is completely out of mode with the faith of the New Testament. In this error, as in most others, there lies a certain amount of truth imperfectly understood."

We are certainly aware that salvation initially is a decision that is once for all time. Often, in eagerness to have people believe, too much human pressure is mixed with the exhorting and as a result, people are often frightened or humanly pushed into an emotional response to what a person has said rather than having truly been dealt with by God's Word and the Holy Spirit. The result is evident as emphasis is placed too heavily on human experience rather than the work and promise of God by which we are saved and have our assurance.

As Tozer concludes,

"...instant Christianity is twentieth century orthodoxy"

There are many dry wells of human error in the realms of our "methodeia," and we that are the witnesses of the faith should not be less than bold in our faithfulness to proclaim the Gospel of Jesus Christ. What then should be our method when there is so much perversion all around us?

J.I Packer speaks clearly to our need to evangelize,

> "So in the last analysis, there is only one method of evangelism: namely, the faithful explanation and application of the Gospel message. From which it follows, and this is the key principle which we are seeking, that the test for any proposed strategy, technique or style of evangelistic action must be this: Will it in fact serve the Word? Is it calculated to be a means of explaining the Gospel truly and fully and applying it deeply and exactly? To the extent to which it tends to overlay and obscure the realities of the message, and to blunt the edge of their application, it is ungodly and wrong."

The next and needful question is, "What then is the proper definition of evangelism?" It is true that often the message is lost in the method, or the method obscures the message. If we are to serve the Word, then just what is that Word?

Packer writes,

> *"How then should evangelism be defined? The New Testament's answer is very simple. According to the New Testament, evangelism is just preaching the Gospel by the evangel. It is a work of communication in which Christians make themselves mouthpieces for God's message of mercy to sinners. Anyone who faithfully delivers that message in a small meeting, from a pulpit, or in a private conversation is evangelizing."*

The theology of that message has been shared in the early chapters. The times are urgent and every believer-witness-ambassador must be a faithful witness to the Gospel of Jesus Christ with boldness and clarity. Thus those who have been drinking from stagnant wells and are seeking living water may find ready relief from their burden of sin and a true understanding of the Gospel of Christ. We must identify stagnant wells and mark them so that those "who truly thirst may drink of the water of life and never thirst again."

It was this very morning that I spoke with a young man thirty years of age, who years ago, under a tremendous emotional impact and a sense of guilt, "walked the aisle," was water baptized and joined the local church. He now looks back from the wilderness of sin and degradation that he has walked in these years, including prison, and does not discern the Biblical truth concerning grace or salvation in which he was supposedly a participant. In his own confession, there has been no work of God at all in his life. He now has only to look back on a fragile, broken empty decision, but no salvation.

Our associate pastor speaks often of his five water baptism experiences and the absolute misery of no assurance and no work of God until his last conviction of sin was dealt with by a faithful pastor who introduced him to the assurance of salvation as revealed in Scripture. It was from that point that his life took root in the truths of Scripture as the Holy Spirit magnified the Word in his life. It was only after several years of Bible College that he finally overcame the scars and the agony of such a brand of instant Christianity and shallow religious experiences that majored on guilt and emotional release, rather than grace and the promises of God. The "what you see is what you get" mentality has led us down a path of spiritual confusion to a cosmetic surface relationship with evangelism and the great truths of Scripture.

I think often of the Scripture that declares,

> *"Man looks on the outward appearance, but the Lord looks on the heart."*

Because this is true, we who have been so external in our emphasis on salvation have reaped what we have sown. This is very sad, for we are left with many decisions, but few disciples. There is much to do and life is so brief, thus we must be about our task as true witnesses of the gospel of Jesus Christ.

John Miller challenges us to be bold witnesses for Christ as he writes,

> *"What we seek, in short, is to get enough truth before men in a personal, loving manner that they may see their responsibility to act before the hour of opportunity has past. A witness empowered by Biblical boldness is clear, compassionate, confrontational and confident; confident that the Holy Spirit, who inspired the testimony, will also apply it to the hearts of those who hear."*

We must always remember that salvation is God's work. God's Word, prayer and the work of the Holy Spirit will always produce God's result. The faithful believer-witness is simply that instrument whereby men hear the Gospel and are saved. Some will water and some will sow, but God will always give the increase.

Isaiah spoke the Word of God when he declared,

> *"For as the rain and the snow come down from heaven, and do not return there without watering the earth, and*

making it bear and sprout and furnishing seed to the sower and bread to the eater; so shall My Word which goes forth from My Mouth; it shall not return to Me empty, without accomplishing what I desire, and without succeeding in the matter for which I send it."

Thank God that as believers it is that which we see with the "eye of faith" that we truly see and then receive.

Part 3

THE LIFE

SPIRITUAL LIFE IS A DIFFERENT KIND OF LIFE. IT IS THE REAL CORE OF EACH PERSON. GOD, WHO IN THE BEGINNING GAVE LIFE, IS THE ONLY ONE WHO CAN ADDRESS THAT KIND OF LIFE. THIS CORE IS THE CENTER OF ABUNDANT LIFE WHICH IS ALSO ETERNAL. THESE CHAPTERS WILL ADDRESS THAT WHICH MAKES THIS KIND OF LIFE POSSIBLE AND OUR INTERACTION WITH IT POSSIBLE. SCRIPTURE DECLARES THAT, "JESUS GIVES US THE GIFT OF LIFE AND LIFE ABUNDANTLY"! IT IS THE GIFT OF HIS RIGHTEOUSNESS.

CHAPTER 15

THE PASSPORT

Every traveler in a foreign country must carry on his person a passport that shows that he is traveling in that place with permission and approval of his government. God, the eternal Father-Creator of all things has demanded that to be joined to His heavenly city, we must meet his absolute standard of righteousness. If we do not, we shall never sojourn there. Man is in no way qualified in and of himself for this high standard for entrance. The whole truth of redemption concerns itself with God making mankind qualified for entrance into that city whose founder and maker is God.

It is the Christ of history, the Messiah, Immanuel, and God with us, who has purchased, by His grace and forgiveness, the believer's passport. By His grace alone is fallen man able to become a citizen of that heavenly city. Upon our acceptance of His generous payment for sin, we are declared righteous. At that moment, we receive our eternal passport! From then on we can never be fully at home on this fallen planet.

We have become by imputed righteousness, aliens and strangers in a foreign land. It is the believer's constant battle with this alien world system and our old nature that causes our greatest HURT. For we are now children of God and joint heirs with Jesus Christ; sealed with the Holy Spirit of promise. Positionally and literally we are no longer our own, "but are bought with a price."

Now as aliens and strangers here on earth, we are commanded to abstain from fleshly lusts which wage war against the soul. Thus, all believers stand in the righteousness of God with a new citizenship. Our passport is grace on the basis of faith and our citizenship is in Heaven from whence comes strength and help.

Paul declared it thusly,

> *"For through Him we both [Jew and Gentiles] have our access in one Spirit to the Father. So then you are no longer strangers and aliens, but you are fellow citizens with the saints, and are God's household."*

Our divine passport daily declares us His children. In this world system of flesh and temporariness, there is a constant battle going on between our two natures. Our old nature is prone to cling to the old ways and the old days. The delicacies of the flesh are on every hand, and we are constantly reminded that "flesh and blood cannot inherit the Kingdom of God." This spiritual warfare!

Our flesh is of earthly-earth and grave-bound. The curse of Adam, after the fall, as he fell under condemnation reminds us that "from dust we came and to dust we shall return." Our endless conflict in this body is that we are "heaven bound" yet earthbound. Our passport is marked "heaven," and our feet walk the earth.

With Paul the Apostle we can sing his song

> *"I have been crucified with Christ; and it is no longer I who live, but Christ lives in me; and the life that I now live in the flesh, I live by faith in the son of God, who loved me and delivered Himself up for me."*

We, as believers, are all pilgrims who are seeking that more substantial city whose founder and builder is God. We are still locked inside a human body that finds itself quite at home in the here and now. Our affections are often captured by the allurements of this planet. Our senses and appetites are always gnawing at our new nature.

Often we are caught in a struggle of affections that leave us "loving this present evil world" more than we should.   Often things that are spiritual become as fantasy while the things of earth become a demanding reality.

A.W Tozer describes this incredible pilgrim as follows,

"The Christian believes that in Christ he has died, yet he is more alive than before; and he fully expects to live forever. He walks on earth while seated in Heaven, and though born on earth, he finds that after his conversion he is not at home here. Like the Nighthawk, which in the air is the essence of grace and beauty, but on the ground is awkward and ugly, so the Christian appears at his best in the heavenly places, but does not fit well into the ways of the very society into which he was born."

Therefore, our passport to eternal life in Jesus Christ makes us pilgrims who are exhorted to be witnesses for Christ. As witnesses we sow and water the seed of the Gospel of Jesus Christ. It is God alone who gives the increase, the harvest of souls. Before we can become a pilgrim, we ourselves must hold a passport to eternal life, our salvation by God's love and grace.

True evangelism is not that which is given to one who is great in natural gifts and talents but rather to the simple pilgrim. Christ has put within us eternal life by the passport of grace and we now live our earthly life under a different name and a different flag. Self-declared believers never give witness to Christ because their passport is forged or counterfeit. They travel under false pretenses. Somewhere in their understanding they thought that they could depend on good works and best efforts by which they would stand credible before the Father. This is a false passport of hope-so instead of hope.

Our world today is filled with religious busy-bodies or activists who seek to satisfy the spirit within by the works of the flesh. One, having never known the Gospel of Christ, cannot share it with another. One can never come back from where he has never been. Our passport is provided by the Father-Creator who gives life, having declared all men guilty, yet seeking to save that which is lost by declaring those who believe as being righteous through Jesus Christ.

Apostle Paul declared to the Romans,

> *"What does the Scripture say? "And Abraham believed God, and it was reckoned to him as righteousness." Now to the one who works, his wage is not reckoned as a favor, but as what is due. But to the one who does not work, but believes in Him who justifies the ungodly, his faith is reckoned righteousness."*

Without a proper passport, we cannot be evangels of His truth, for we must have the truth to give the truth. Perhaps this is that fly in the ointment within the organized church of our time. Far too many people have identified with the church, which have come by way of decision, but have never been spiritually regenerated. Thus, thousands have joined our churches, but have no passport to eternal life. It is a sad fact, but history is simply being repeated as an unregenerate membership practices a "form of godliness while denying the power thereof."

There can be no pilgrims and no sojourns without that divine passport that provides power and witness. Thus, the modern church is often filled with those who are as alien to the things of God as they are friends of the world system. This is not a new innovation, for fallen mankind has always made up its own rules for righteousness.

The self-righteous have always declared their works as being adequate for salvation. Yet, without the passport of grace, they are eternally lost. This reality should thrust the true believer into the world to declare faithfully the good news of God's love that provides for those who believe, a passport to eternal life. Obadiah Holmes, a 17th century martyr, stood against the religious and institutional faithlessness of his day and declared that which we have need of hearing today.

He said,

> *"There is simply no substitute for conversion—not works, not righteousness, not worthy ancestry, not good repute among men. Only a single way remains....your work is only and alone to accept the proffer of free grace in and through Jesus Christ, and to be converted. That is to be truly turned into the Lord, both in heart and conversation (life), old things become done away and all things become new."*

THIS ALONE IS OUR PASSPORT!

CHAPTER 16

THE PILGRIM!

The Apostle Peter declared the following:

> *"But you are a chosen race, a royal priesthood, a holy nation, a people for God's own possession, that you may proclaim the excellencies of Him, who has called you out of darkness into His marvelous light; for you once were not a people, but now you are the people of God; you have not received mercy, by now you have received mercy. Beloved, I urge you are aliens and strangers to abstain from fleshly lusts, which wage war against your soul."*

The dictionary says that a pilgrim is a traveler from foreign parts. As believers, our passports have been issued by God's grace. We have been called out of darkness to this land of passing day. We have been sealed by the Holy Spirit and we are in transition under subjection to God's command and providence. Our travel is not without hazards, trials, often defeat and setbacks; but it is nonetheless ordained of God. We are destined for that which has been prepared for us by His grace. We walk in the light and work in the dark!

The Apostle Paul declared:

"He chose us in Him before the foundation of the world, that we should be holy and blameless before Him in love."

Our journey began the moment we believed; and our destination has been set, our passport issued. Now we "walk by faith not by sight." We are indeed pilgrims, aliens and strangers, a part of the Heavenly City, on the basis of faith.

John Edgar, who edited all the works of John Bunyan, who gave us the immortal "Pilgrim's Progress," wrote,

"The pilgrimage of life is a deeply interesting subject, co-existent with human nature; every individual of our race is upon pilgrimage, from the cradle to the grave. It is the progress of the soul through time to enter upon a boundless eternity; beset on all sides, at every avenue, and at every moment, with spiritual foes of the deepest subtlety, journeying from the commencement to the close of the course through an enemy's country, uncertain of the term of existence, certain only that it must terminate and usher into an eternal state, either of exquisite happiness or awful misery. All mankind are pilgrims; all are pressing through this world; the Christian willingly considers that his life is a journey because he is seeking a better country; but the multitudes are anxious to prevent the recollection, that time is a preparation for eternity, and in the consequence of their neglect, they shudder when

approaching the brink of the grave, into which they are irresistibly plunged."

The small and important vessel that is used to pass cool, refreshing water that has come from the deep of the well by the drawing bucket to our lips is the "dipper." It is our responsibility, as believer-pilgrims to faithfully pass the living water of the Gospel to those who thirst for the truth. As "dippers" of truth, we must be clean vessels and faithful to that which we are commissioned to do. As faithful pilgrims, we should never forget that we are a "royal priesthood." Of all the truths for the believer, this particular truth declares our most cherished position in grace.

Paul told Timothy that there was only one mediator between God and man and that was the man, Christ Jesus. As believers, we each have access to the Father directly and constantly. Therefore, we are commanded "to come boldly to the throne of grace, that we may find grace to help in time of need." We all go there when we HURT!

As sons of God and children of God, we stand forgiven, enabled to come directly into our Heavenly Father's presence. We are never to be under another's domination and control, for we are His alone.

In our time, we have majored much on the corporate communion of believers with one another and with God. Yet we have neglected too often that most vital individual connection of Father-child, the "priesthood of the believer." Never will there be a proper communion among the saints until each and every believer-pilgrim exercises his own priesthood before the Father. For it is by the exercising of this function that we become all that He desires us to be.

There must be true union with the Father before there can be common union between brothers and sisters in Christ. When this understanding is weak, the individual pilgrim will never be strong and able to do battle with enemies of his faith.

True evangelism, which is the faithful proclamations of the Gospel, is brought about by the growth of the believer-pilgrim who faithfully responds to the position of the believer-priest. If the believer does not understand this relationship to the Father, his growth and witness will be retarded and inadequate.

Peter spoke,

> *"Ye also as living stones are being built up as a spiritual house for a holy priesthood, to offer up spiritual sacrifices acceptable to God through Jesus Christ."*

Jerry Haughton speaks clearly to the process of growth in the believer-priest's life,

> *"It seems that most believer-priests have difficulty in realizing and facing up to the fact that the Spirit does not rush to complete His development of their Christian life. So many feel they are not making progress unless they are swiftly and constantly moving ahead."*

Because this is true, the baby believer-pilgrim must learn to depend upon the Spirit and the Word of God and not be distracted by lesser matters. We must learn to filter all things through the Word of God and learn to discern those who are faithful to the Truth and those who are not. We must learn again and again to bring all teachings into line with God's Word and allow nothing to take the place of the direct relationship with God and His Word in his life. Every believer should realize that much time is required to grow and that we can have confidence in God's ability alone to discipline us, mature us and work in us to His glory.

Paul exhorted the Philippians with this promise,

> *"Being confident of this very thing, that He which has begun a good work in you will perform it until the day of Jesus Christ."*

Haughton continues,

> *"Since the believer-priest matures by the principle of appropriating the promises of the Word so that they become experiences of daily living, much time is necessary for healthy growth. Unless the time factor is acknowledged from both the mind and heart, there is always danger of turning to the false enticement of short-cuts in Christian growth through means of certain experiences and special blessings where one becomes pathetically bond to changing feelings and neglectful Biblical facts."*

It is the growing pilgrim-believer who will become in God's own time a true witness to the Gospel. True Biblical evangelism has been impeded by misinformed, unhealthy and malnourished believers. Many believers have been dominated by stifling programs and personality-centered ministries that have failed to rightly demonstrate, by teaching and life, the divinely decreed "priesthood of the believer."

Where the believer-pilgrim has not been rightly taught our proper function before God, we can surely have no proper understanding of our function and the declaration of the Gospel. A spiritually unhealthy believer makes for an unhealthy witness.

Ray Stedman speaks to this problem as follows,

> *"Great damage has been done by unhealthy saints attempting to reach out to the world in evangelism or social help in spasms of dedicated zeal but without true spiritual health. Burdened with unsolved problems in their own lives, and unconsciously displaying unresolved hypocrisies of prejudice and outlook, their spasmodic activities in evangelism or help seem to be hollow mockeries of Christianity in the eyes of those they hope to reach."*

We must learn, as teaching elders. pastors and believer-witnesses that those who would be discipled as believers must learn to maintain their "priesthood." This is of primary importance and not just an idea that sounds spiritual. Each and every believer-pilgrim can discover what God has so lovingly provided for him if he will faithfully study what Scripture teaches.

We are taught, as believers, that we, each one, are "ministers of reconciliation" and are gifted by the Holy Spirit in our pilgrimage to minister in some way to the whole of the body of Christ.

Concerning this truth, Jon Zens writes,

> *"All believers are 'ministers' [believer-priests] who have been gifted by God so that they may lovingly build up their spiritual brothers and sisters…each Christian has received a spiritual gift… a gift is a special ability given graciously by God to each person in Christ's body to help others toward spiritual maturity."*

In conclusion, we must state once again that the work of the believer-pilgrim-priest is a witness and should be manifest as he/she walks with the Lord and grows in grace. Thus, in time, one will be found able and faithful in proclaiming the Gospel, trusting the harvest to the Father, who so graciously honors the "seed" of the Word.

Once again, it should be stated that the work of evangelism is not the work of some articulate super-witness. Rather it is the commission of every believer in the pilgrimage from life to death, from earth to that eternal city where we look to the author and finisher of our faith. We know that He is faithful and, according to His Word, He will guide our frail boat into that eternal harbor of the soul.

Surely we can say with the Psalmist,

"Thy statutes are the house of my pilgrimage."

CHAPTER 17

THE WORD BECOMES FLESH!

"In the beginning was the Word, and the Word was with God, and the Word was God. He was in the beginning with God. And the Word became flesh, and dwelt among us, and we beheld His glory, the glory as of the only begotten from the Father, full of grace and truth. And you shall know the truth and the truth shall make you free."

The written Word of God is that revealed Word that was given by the Holy Spirit to those who were guided by Him. Through the vehicle of human personality, God gave us His written revelation that was not an act of human will or opinion but came from God. As the Holy Spirit conceived Jesus Christ in the womb of Mary so the Word of God was so conceived by the Holy Spirit in the minds of those chosen vessels. This is a most important understanding for the believer-priest-pilgrim. Without settling the question of Scriptural authority the believer will be forever unstable. God's revealed, written Word has been given for our spiritual maintenance and nothing else can take its place in our lives.

Paul, in speaking to Timothy, stated very clearly its purpose in our lives as he declared,

> *"All Scripture is inspired by God and is profitable for teaching, for reproof, for correction, for training in righteousness; that the man of God may be adequate, and equipped for every good work."*

To waver or be double-minded concerning the authority and inspiration of Scripture is to be always immature without "any sure Word of prophecy," easily blown to and fro, driven by "every wind of doctrine."

Harold Lindsell speaks to the matter as he writes the following,

> *"C.S. Lewis, in <u>Mere Christianity</u>, says something that is helpful. 'Man needs something he hasn't got and God puts it in him.' By way of illustration, he mentions a child being taught to write. He says, '...you hold its hand while it forms the letters; that is, it forms the letters because you are forming them. So with Scripture, as fallible, limited human beings sat down to write what they wanted to write, because they wanted to write (but could not by themselves) what the Holy Spirit wanted written. Inspiration was not mechanical, i.e., the writers were not secretaries, who wrote what was dictated to them. If the words are congruent with the ideas, the words no less than the ideas take on great significance. In the Bible, sometimes a single word makes all the difference about what is to be conveyed...So, even the*

words (verbal inspiration) are an integral part of inspiration."

The evangel is absolutely dependent upon the Word of God. God's honoring of His Word declares not what we think, speculate or opine concerning what He said. We must never forget that man honors man, but God honors His Word. As man/woman is faithful in proclaiming and giving witness to that Word, they receive the blessing of being an instrument of the Word. Thus, the written Word takes on flesh as we believer-witnesses believe, know and live out that truth.

Paul commanded us to,

> *"Study to show thyself approved unto God a workman that needeth not to be ashamed, rightly dividing the Word of truth."*

In living what we know, we bear truth in our bodies that we are "temples of the Holy Spirit," and because this is so, the truth lives. We are commissioned by Scripture to "walk in the Spirit," and to be "filled with the Spirit." We are, by the Spirit enabled to speak the Gospel with power and authority, for it alone is "the power of God unto salvation."

The psalmist declared,

> *"The law of the Lord is perfect, restoring the soul; the testimony of the Lord is sure, making wise the simple."*

The Word of God, as revealed in Scripture, is without question the "plenary, verbal, inerrant Word of God." This simply means that in the original manuscripts, the Scriptures are the full, complete, perfect revelation from God to man! To play word games concerning this truth, clouds the issue, glorifies man and detracts from the Gospel message.

Before we can be an effective witness, we must know the Biblical message and the Holy Spirit who empowers it. We can have absolute confidence that no Word of His will ever return void, but will accomplish that for which it is sent. This does not require a formal, theological education or great human ability. Rather, it requires a knowledge of God's Word and a faithful proclamation of the same, in order that men might hear and believe.

> *"For faith comes by hearing and hearing by the Word of God."*

We are living in strange times where spiritual pilgrims, believer-ambassadors, find themselves in conflict concerning the Word of God. Never has so much verbiage and discussion, fear and suspicion, come forth from supposedly brothers in the faith who stand on opposite sides of that which should unify us rather than divide us. How sad! We use names like liberal and conservative because there are those who have positioned themselves at odds with the absolute credibility of inerrant Scripture.

This causes the unbeliever to be even more confused as he views the contemporary church. We must "rightly divide the Word of Truth" as well as properly believe and live the truths of God's Word. If we are to be faithful witnesses of the Gospel of Jesus Christ, we must stand absolutely unwavering upon the credibility, inspiration and authority of God's Word.

Francis Schaeffer writes with understanding to this issue:

> "When those who claim to be God's people turn aside from the Word of God and from the Christ of history, this is more heinous in the sight of God than the worst case of infidelity in marriage, for it destroys the reality, the great central bridegroom-bride relationship. Consider the liberal theology of our day. It denies the personal God who is there. It denies the Bible as God's verbalized Word. It denies God's way of salvation. The liberals elevate their own humanistic theories to a position above the Word of God, the revealed communication of God to men. They make gods which

are no gods, but are merely the projection of their own minds."

Because this is so, we should never take lightly the Word of God in our own lives. The Word must become alive in us, in our minds, lives and lifestyles by which we communicate who we really are. God's Word must become flesh and blood in us, for we are "temples of the Holy Spirit." The natural man does not understand the message of the Gospel. Nor do those who have become enemies of the Gospel. The Gospel is the power of God unto salvation.

Robert L. Saucy says it this way,

"The effectiveness of the Word of God in producing salvation explains the many attempts of the enemy to eliminate the Bible. In the narrow sense, the Gospel focuses on the death of Christ for our sins and His triumphant resurrection. (I Corinthians 15:1-4) In a broader sense, however, the whole of Scripture including the revelation of our sinful condition and God's solution may be said to be the Gospel. For apart from the light of God's Word exposing our lost estate, the revelation of the work of Christ would be meaningless. Thus, the Bible totally is God's Word. He plants it as a spiritual seed into the hearts of those who receive it."

We, believing pilgrims who would be faithful witnesses, remember the words of Christ when He said,

"Sanctify them in the truth; Thy Word is truth."

The truth of God and His Word are parts of each other, and to attack His Word is to attack Him. Throughout history, men have fallen into dangerous positions as they arrogantly modify and even change the truth, feeling free to give their scholarship equal billing with the very Word of God. This amounts to spiritual adultery.

The Bible was not written for professional theologians but for the common man who would be enlightened by the Holy Spirit to salvation, then the truths of discipleship. We, as sojourners in a foreign land, must give ourselves relentlessly to the study of Scripture allowing nothing to come between its truth and our lives in either belief or lifestyle.

Tim LaHaye captures this insight when he writes,

> *"Unfortunately most Christians have the idea they cannot understand the Bible. They think it was written for theologians or ministers, so all they do is listen to 'Bible scholars' lecture and preach or read books about the Bible, but spend very little time studying it for themselves. The thing that is so sad about this is, that the Bible wasn't written for theologians, it was written for people just like you and me! Once the fact that you can study the Bible yourself really grips you, your Christian life will take on an entirely new dimension."*

If God's Word is to become flesh in each of us as pilgrim-believers we must stand firmly for the absolute authority of His Word and for the power that its understanding produces in our lives. Our lives will then faithfully give witness to His grace.

Arthur Pink reminds us,

> *"Surrender the dogma of verbal inspiration and you are left like a rudderless ship on a stormy sea, at the mercy of every wind that blows. Deny that the Bible is, without any qualification, the very Word of God, and you are left without any supreme authority."*

It is absolutely essential that every believer comes to realize how urgent it is that we affirm daily our confidence in God's Word. We do this by determination to study the Scriptures daily, seek and apply them to our lives. Many believers have been far too lax in this matter. There can be no true discipleship or faithful witness without much attention being given to the Scriptures. Only as we take heed to this truth within the scope of our daily lives will the world ever witness the Word becoming flesh in and through us.

Paul declared,

"But we have this treasure in earthen vessels that the surpassing greatness of the power may be of God and not from ourselves.

CHAPTER 18

DISCIPLESHIP

A disciple is a learner. A disciple of Christ is one who knows Him as his/her personal Savior. The Believer is never given the option as to whether he will be a disciple or not. By the very nature of our calling in Jesus Christ "before the foundation of the world," we are declared disciples. The early churches clearly understood that a believer was to be a disciple.

This is very obvious in the treatment of Paul by the other disciples after his conversion. The Scriptures declare concerning his appearance at Jerusalem,

> *"And when he had come to Jerusalem, he was trying to associate with the disciples; and they were all afraid of him, not believing that he was a disciple."*

The implication is that if he was not a disciple, he was not a believer. They were, in fact, questioning his having believed.

It was our Lord Jesus Christ, who commissioned His followers after His resurrection and before His ascension as follows,

"All authority has been given to Me in heaven and on earth. Go therefore and make disciples of all the nations, baptizing them in the name of the Father and the Son and the Holy Spirit, teaching them to observe all that I commanded you; and lo I am with you always, even to the end of the age."

Discipleship is a matter of obedience and with our salvation it becomes our responsibility and that enables us by the Holy Spirit to be obedient to Christ. Discipleship is the bringing of our every thought into obedience to Christ, "pressing on to the high calling of God in Jesus Christ."

Paul put it this way,

"We are destroying speculations and every lofty thing raised up against the knowledge of God, and we are taking every thought captive to the obedience of Christ."

Obedience is that which manifests God's kind of love in both our talk and our walk. True discipleship therefore is obedience in action, manifesting His kind of Divine Love in our service to others.

Someone has said it this way,

"Questions of how to conduct oneself as a Christian, or how to serve as a Christian, must be answered by life itself, the life of the individual in his direct, responsible relationship to God. This is a dynamic, never a static

thing. And how can we speak at all of the true meaning of conduct and service, if we do not speak first and last of life? It is love, which sums up all other commands. Therefore, he is the one who knows better than anyone else how to conduct himself, and how to serve the one he loves. Love prescribes an answer in a given situation, as no mere rule can do. The man whose life is lived in love does, in fact, live in God and God does, in fact, live in him."

To be more specific, we must apply our discipleship, fulfilling it by obedience and manifesting it in love in life's daily involvements and relationships. This is without doubt our greatest challenge.

It is in daily relationships that we as believers face, as nowhere else, the real issues of life. It is here that rubber hits the road. There is no doubt that amidst the pressures of daily life obedience to the specific commands of Scripture is most difficult. It is not difficult to understand the meaning of the commands given to us, but it is difficult to carry them out with genuine grace.

Dietrich Bonhoeffer says concerning obedience in relationship to discipleship,

"The life of discipleship is not heir-ship that we pay to a good master, but obedience to the Son of God."

Discipleship is not just positive resolve or an inspirational moment that is brought about by good feelings, but a Spirit led and controlled act brought about by our submission to Him.

Bonhoeffer again writes,

> "Jesus knows only one possibility; simple surrender and obedience, not interpreting it or applying it, but doing and obeying it. That is the only way to hear His Word. But again, He does not mean that it is to be discussed as an ideal, He means us to get on with it. The disciple looks solely at his Master. But when a man follows Jesus Christ and bears the image of the incarnate, crucified and risen Lord, when he has become the image of God, we may at last say that he has been called to be the "imitator of God.""

Paul said it this way,

> "Be ye therefore imitators of God, as beloved children, and again, Be imitators of Me."

Natural abilities do not the witness make! Rather, the believer-witness is the product of a supernatural work of grace and Spirit empowerment. True evangelism never rests upon the foundation of the natural, but supernatural. It must be sadly acknowledged that in our times we have settled for the superficial externals and the ability to speak the words of Scripture dramatically without the power of life and Godly character by which the truth of God is lived out in the many aspects of human relationships.

In the realm of family, we who would be faithful witnesses must put the principles of God's Word to the test in our lives as they are spelled out clearly in relation to our responsibility and blessings. The arena of family and kin perhaps forms our greatest challenge for both blessing and frustration. It is here that we stand on the front line of testimony and witness. To fail here is to be weak in our front-line defense.

In these days of family erosion and decay we must, as believers, encourage one another. We are commissioned by God's Word to pray for one another, holding up each other as we fight the enemy of our souls concerning the unity of our families. As believer-disciples in any given community we must be unified in our common commitment to Christ and declare the whole counsel of God concerning His design and order for the family. It is in this relationship that we will discover our greatest victories and our greatest defeats.

The writer of Hebrews speaks of the need to encourage one another as he writes,

"Take care brethren, lest there should be in any one of you an evil, unbelieving heart, in falling away from the living God. But encourage one another day after day, as long as it is still called 'today,' lest any one of you be hardened by the deceitfulness of sin."

True evangelism depends upon the believer's faithfulness to God within his daily relationship. When the family relationship is under attack, we are not long in realizing our own weakness and vulnerability to the "god of this world" and to the "flesh." It is in the home that our sexuality and all that comprises our humanity comes to the surface. We who comprise the family of God must pray daily for our homes. Yet, in the battle for our minds and our allegiance, we must not allow our family and kin to keep us from submission to Christ and discipleship.

Friendship is a word that is often misunderstood and used at times rather loosely. It often refers to a relationship with another person, whether good or bad. Friends often influence our lives for good or bad even more than the home. We, as believers can carelessly cast our lot with those who would distract us from faithful discipleship.

Paul exhorted us this way,

"Do not be deceived; bad company corrupts good morals."

James declared,

"Do you not know that friendship with the world is hostility toward God?"

In application, we should understand that we are to be friends with those who are believers as well as non-believers, yet we must not allow our friendships to bind us so tightly as to weaken our discipleship. Our first obligations in friendship are God-ward. Abraham was known as a friend of God. If we are friends of God, all other friends will find their place in our lives. They will become true friends locked into proper priorities and we will never use them wrongly or love them with misplaced affection. Jesus called us friends and as such all of our friendships will find their proper level as we walk in the discipleship of His friendship.

Each of us believers will, in our lifetimes, be asked to submit to spiritual leadership of some kind and as a witness at least assume some kind of spiritual leadership. Discipleship must enter into these relationships. It is absolutely essential that the believer-disciple seek to be balanced. As followers, we should seek the same balance in being led as we would if we were leading.

Every believer is to be a witness for Christ and thus we, each one, have a reason to be heard. We must learn well to combat our self-righteousness. Any witness who is faithful to speak for Christ, will at some time confront his pride and how easily it can puff him up or tempt him terribly concerning his own goodness and abilities. As witnesses we must be very sensitive to these matters for many a soul has been snared by pride in his attempted faithfulness to the things of God. Even the most timid soul when giving the truth of God finds in that moment of spiritual power a temptation to ride on God's shirttail to a moment of glory or self-righteousness.

Oswald Chambers speaks powerfully to this matter as he writes,

> *"As Christians, workers, worldliness is not our snare, sin is not our snare but spiritual wanting is, taking the pattern and print of the religious age we live in, making eyes at spiritual success. We have the commercial view---so many souls saved and sanctified; thank God, now it is all right. Our work begins where God's grace has laid the foundation; we are not to save souls, but to disciple them. Salvation and sanctification are the work*

of God's sovereign grace; our work as His disciples is to disciple lives until they are wholly yielded to God. One life wholly devoted to God is of more value to God than one hundred lives simply wakened by His Spirit. As workers for God, we must reproduce our own kind of spirituality, and that will be God's witness to us as workers. God brings us to a standard of life by His grace and we are responsible for reproducing that standard in others."

As individual ambassador-witness we must be faithful to God's truth concerning discipleship in every area of our lives. Obviously, there are many relationships with which we have to do and there are many changing relationships with which we find ourselves daily confronted. Our relationship to discipleship must daily be considered.

Paul has addressed this concerning his own witness saying,

"For our gospel did not come to you in word only, but also in power and in the Holy Spirit and with full conviction; just as you know what kind of men we proved to be among you for your sake."

Discipleship is not static, a once in a lifetime commitment, but rather a dynamic discipline by which we, moment by moment, are brought under submission to Jesus Christ during a lifetime.

Paul said,

> *"Being confident of this very thing that He that hath begun a good work in you will perform it until the day of Jesus Christ."*

As Chambers says,

> *"If the closest relationships of life clash with the claims of Jesus Christ, He says it must be instant obedience to Himself. Discipleship means personal passionate devotion to a Person, Our Lord Jesus Christ."*

As disciples, we are His possessions and are responsible to seek His Will in all the relationships of our lives. Every believer is indeed the "called of God," a disciple of Christ, a saint whether weak or strong. It is God alone who makes us His disciples. It is our commission to proclaim the Gospel by the witness of our walk and talk.

Paul declared,

> *"Whether, when you eat or drink or whatever you do, do all to the glory of God."*

We are indeed believer-pilgrim-priest-evangelist-disciples, who by God's divine enablement are empowered to "do all things through Christ which strengthens us."

Chambers speaks to our discipleships as follows,

"If we are to be disciples of Jesus, we must be made disciples supernaturally; as long as we have the dead set purpose of being disciples, we may be sure we are not, 'I have chosen you'. That is the way the grace of God begins. It is a constraint we cannot get away from; we can disobey it, but we cannot generate it. The drawing is done by the supernatural grace of God, and we never can trace where His work begins. Our Lord's making of a disciple is supernatural. He does not build on any natural capacity at all. God does not ask us to do the things that are easy to us naturally; He only asks us to do the things we are perfectly fitted to do by His grace, and the cross will come along that line always."

CHAPTER 19

AMBASSADORS ALL

Webster's unabridged dictionary defines the word ambassador as "the highest diplomatic representative that one sovereign power or state sends officially to another." An ambassador is also an official herald or messenger. Thus, in the days of old, an ambassador "represented one king in the court of another."

William Macomber writes concerning the ambassador as follows,

> "Authority is notably centered in the person of the ambassador, and there is still a marked degree of protocol deference paid to him, both outside and inside his embassy. The deference originated in the day when kings considered themselves anointed by God, and when their ambassadors, as their direct representatives, expected to be treated as nearly-as-August personages. The ambassador still represents his head of state and, more than that, his embassy colleagues consider that through the office he holds, he more than anyone among them symbolizes and represents their country."

It is the ambassador who has the commanding voice as he speaks for his country on the soil of foreign countries to which he is sent. He is the highest in calling of all diplomats. It was the Apostle Paul who referred to himself as an "ambassador in chains" as he proclaimed the Gospel of Jesus Christ.

It is also Paul who gives us to understand that, as believers, we are given the "ministry of reconciliation." This is a ministry of declaring to those under the condemnation of sin and rebellion against God that He has paid their sin debt in His son, Jesus Christ. He did so that they might be "declared righteous," thus reconciled to Him by faith in Jesus Christ.

Paul told the Corinthians that this word of reconciliation was given to them as he charged them,

> *"Therefore, we are ambassadors for Christ, as though God were entreating through us; we beg you on behalf of Christ, be reconciled to God."*

Paul rejected the idea that we should "hustle" or "peddle the Word of God." He declared,

> *"For we are not like many, peddling the Word of God, but as from sincerity, but as from God, we speak in Christ in the sight of God."*

The idea of hustling and peddling often fits into the scheme of modern high pressure sales techniques that prevail these days. Granted, true salesmanship in the classic sense is the representation of a product not the pushing or hustling of a product. If the product is quality it will sell and prove itself. But in a world of poor quality control and an overabundance of products to sell, man has often reverted to high pressure tactics.

"Peddling the Word" implies this mentality. How often this has been done with embellished schemes that pressure people into so-called "decisions for Christ." This is not new for Paul confronted this in his time and clearly separated himself from such mentality. Mankind is susceptible to such schemes and methods because of the guilt and sin that he carries in his unregenerate heart.

Fallen man is ever seeking to reform himself and change his way of living. Human schemes and methods provide him a way of responding to God on his terms. There are also many who minister by seeking to serve God on their terms. Many also minister, seeking to serve God, as they abide by "religious feelings" and "being led." Many fail to realize that God's Word has clearly spoken concerning proper principles of ministry. Because this is so, those with itching ears have been able to secure for themselves men who will scratch were they itch.

It is a sad commentary indeed on contemporary Christendom, wherein a theology of convenience prevails or "if it works its right" and "success at any price." The vocabulary of "modern evangelism" is sometimes comprised of such words as successful, decision, competition, statistics, dynamic, exciting and effective. These words in and of themselves are positive words; but when coupled with the mind of the "hustler" they imply the "how much" and "how many" of external measurement. Such words can reflect a fleshy "can you top this?" mentality that majors on the externals of evangelism rather than the "newness of life" and the grace of God.

In the name of such externalized evangelism, some have "baptized paganism" while using the words of Scripture. Many have had their minds and hearts assaulted by using self-serving human methodology, of which even the modern secular ambassador would never approve.

We should be reminded at this point that the Greek word "methodeia" is the word from which we get the word method. Paul spoke of this as craftiness, the implication being that men in their impatience and drive for results determine to produce results their way. This often happens because of the nature of man's pride that wants to credit himself and be credited by others as righteous and effective.

We all know these feelings. Such leaders and teachers have chosen in their own energy to get results by "the trickery of men, by creativeness (methodeia) in deceitful scheming."

As "**AMBASSADORS FOR CHRIST"** we must give ourselves to the very highest of motives and methods being very careful not to be a stumbling block to weaker brothers or a wall of resistance to the unbeliever (outsider) who is most critical and without understanding.

Paul spelled out the heart of an ambassador for Christ as he wrote to the Colossians,

> *"Devote yourself to prayer, keeping alert in it with an attitude of thanksgiving; praying at the same time for us as well, that God may open up to us a door for the Word, so that we may speak forth the mystery of Christ, for which I have also been imprisoned; in order that I may make it clear [the Gospel] in the way I ought to speak. Conduct yourselves with wisdom toward outsiders [unbelievers], making the most of the opportunity. Let your speech always be with grace, seasoned as it were, with salt, so that you may know how you should respond to each person [believer or unbeliever]."*

These are the words of a "true ambassador" if you please, a "divine" describes the pattern of work and witness for life and lip as concisely and to the point as any in Scripture. We must realize that modern diplomacy and the work of a secular ambassador often calls for compromises and positions that would not befit a believer-ambassador.

Little has been written concerning Paul's "Ambassadorial Evangelism." But within its context lies the key to true Biblical evangelism. Books on contemporary diplomacy offer much insight into this most important position of ambassador. Paul was not a pusher but a prodder and most certainly not a salesman, but an "ambassador for Christ."

Though modern diplomacy has produced some scandals and tragedies there is still much to learn from the high standard that the world sets for its diplomats. Most of them are older, experienced, energetic, responsible and flexible. They do not make policy; they represent the policy and principles of the sovereign nation that sends them forth. We can learn much from them and the requirements that are placed upon their lives. Many of the core qualities of the modern ambassador are transferable to the believer-ambassador.

William Macomber, in <u>A Handbook of Modern Diplomacy,</u> lists the four "core qualities" of a modern diplomat as follows:

(1) **Integrity**: *"Morality aside, it just does not pay to be deceitful. The short-term benefits occasionally garnered by such a practice are outweighed by the consequences of discovery and in the end there is nearly always discovery. As so many writers on diplomacy have pointed out, a reputation for lack of integrity will follow a diplomat around the earth, and once appended to him, he will be suspect at all capitals and his usefulness will be ended. He cannot function unless every day he performs each task in a way which will continue to meet the confidence of both his host country and his own. A true diplomat will cultivate and guard nothing more zealously than a reputation for honorable dealing"*

(2) **Discretion**: *"Discretion is first of all required in a diplomat's dealing with colleagues of their nations. Carelessness can do serious, often critical damage to both. Responsible diplomats will always be guarded in what they say to each other, with those of his government and those of another. Of all the areas in which a diplomat faces the challenge of discretion, none is more important or more difficult than his dealings with the press. He must never forget their right to know and critically view his life. He must learn to be frank, helpful and accurate, but never careless and never indiscreet. In his dealings with both the press and other diplomats, he must also remember always that indiscretions come about in part, as well as in whole,*

that a fragmentary indiscretion can be as damaging as the whole."

(3) **Energy, which means zeal:** *A diplomat also learns early in the game that health and stamina require abstemious self-discipline as far as food and drink are concerned. Energy also requires zeal and classic advice all diplomats know; keep a low profile, observe and report. John Kenneth Galbraith, former ambassador, declared that what diplomacy requires is 'the clear-headed determined operator who knows what should be done and has a strong desire to do it'."*

(4) **Self-discipline:** *"This means more than a capacity for calm, and for controlling one's frustrations and emotions under difficult circumstances. Even more important, it means control of one's ego. For particularly with senior diplomats, the problem of vanity can be the most deadly – the more so because it is a quiet, malignant disease, often unrecognized by those in its grip. For the value of a diplomat's judgment declines in direct proportion to the degree he permits his ego to invade the processes of that judgement. Finally, most diplomats assume that they have come to their profession with an inherent commitment to each of these critical core qualities of the bona fide diplomat. They soon find, however, that in the stresses and complexities of their professions, these qualities are far easier to believe in than to adhere to. Put another way, believing in them on the one hand and instilling them in one's character and performance are quite different propositions. The latter is an endless task, one the*

diplomat must pursue from the day he enters his profession to the day he leaves it."

Need more be said? The position of **AMBASSADOR** is one of great seriousness and responsibility. Paul told the Corinthians that "we are ambassadors for Christ" and that "we" is "us" and that "us" is every believer. It would help each of us to read again and again these "core qualities" and pray that we will allow the Holy Spirit to make application in our needy lives. At the same time, we must search the Scriptures so that we would be enlightened to our "ambassadorial" responsibilities.

We are either weak or strong in our faith, depending on our maturity. By His grace we have been justified and sanctified and by that same grace we must grow up in Him. We must be faithful to His divinely given textbook for growth, "His Word," by which we will be "thoroughly furnished unto every good work." Our "core qualities" should reflect Christ as the core of our lives. We are His alone.

Oswald Chambers writes,

> *"Our Lord makes a disciple His own possession, He becomes responsible for him. 'Ye shall be witnesses unto Me.' The spirit that comes in is not that of doing*

anything for Jesus, but of being a perfect delight to Him. The secret of the missionary (ambassador) is I am His, and He is carrying out His enterprises through me. Be entirely His."

Once we have declared for Christ the world becomes all the more critical of what we say and do. We are in a hostile and foreign land as "children of God" and are commissioned as believer-ambassadors. The natural man often sets higher standards for his human enterprises than we who know the "King of Kings." God forgive us!

God is Sovereign and we represent His Glory. Heaven is our Home. His Word is our handbook, and His Spirit is our "enabler" and "teacher." It is Him ALONE whom we represent and His message that we proclaim.

Scripture says,

> *"For faith cometh by hearing and hearing by the Word of God."*

We must,

> *"Study to show yourselves approved unto God, workmen [believer - pilgrim - priest - evangelist -*

ambassadors] who need not be ashamed, rightly dividing the Word of truth."

It has been said that angels were the first ambassadors or diplomats in that they delivered the message of God to man; but now we, as believers, are the messengers of God and empowered by the Holy Spirit; for we ARE ambassadors for Christ! We, as believers are meant to be handlers of the Word of Life – "Holy Dippers" indeed!

The songwriter has stated it well in one of the hymns of my childhood, which I recall with fond memories. It is entitled, "The King's Business".

"I am a stranger here, within a foreign land;

My home is far away, upon a golden strand

Ambassador to be of realms beyond the sea,

I'm here on business for my King."

CHAPTER 20

SAYS WHO?

There are times when a person is allowed to say most anything and get by with it whether what is said is true or false. One of those areas of privilege is tombstones. For years I have enjoyed the fun and novelty of reading tombstones. Somehow, they reflect one's individuality and mortality as nothing else can. Graveyards, both large and small, are alive with history. The yesteryear comes alive with pithy statements that are etched on pieces of granite. I recently was given a book of epitaphs that illustrate the point. A tombstone out of the old west from the 1880's tells it all,

"Here lies Butch

We planted him raw

He was quick on the trigger

But slow on the draw."

And another one that is brief and to the point from a cemetery near Cripple Creek, Colorado,

"He called Bill Smith a liar."

In North Cemetery in Nantucket, Massachusetts, engraved on a small slate stone, is found this thought,

"Under the sod, under these trees;

Lies the body of Jonathan Pease,

He is not here, only his pod

He has shelled out his peas

And gone to his God."

Finally, one that may be more fiction than fact, but is very amusing. It is engraved on a dear lady's gravestone,

"I told you I was sick!"

In such places as graveyards, it matters not what one might say or believe. What difference does it make? The tragic truth is that we have allowed the same kind of tolerance to exist in relation to the things that are eternal that make all of the difference in the world. Physical death is not an ending but the beginning of eternal life or eternal death. As we walk the earth in our corruptible bodies we often fail to comprehend the seriousness of eternal decisions that are made this side of the grave.

We are exposed daily to many statements about God and His Word and often, if honest and knowledgeable, we should declare, "Says who?" "Show me!" By what authority are men speaking? They tamper with the Gospel message by which men pass from life unto death. We, as believer-witnesses are indeed "holy dippers" in the sense that we handle the Word of God. We are also believer-disciples under obedience.

Paul declared with divine authority,

> *"So then, my beloved, just as you have always obeyed not as in my presence only, but now in my absence, work out your own salvation with fear and trembling; for it is God who is at work in you both to will and to work for His good pleasure. Do all things without grumbling or disputing; that you prove yourselves to be blameless and innocent, children of God above reproach, in the midst of a crooked and perverse generation, among whom you appear as lights in the world."*

The authority of our souls must never be a conglomerate of personal opinion, public sentiment or theology double-talk. Our commission is too great, the hour is too late and we have little time for those who would change our orders and tailor our thinking so that we become "holy dippers" that cannot carry faithfully the water of life from the well of life to the thirsty who seek it.

Jesus said to the woman at the well of Sychar concerning the water of life,

> *"But whoever drinks of the water I shall give him shall never thirst; but the waters that I shall give him shall become in him a well of water springing up to eternal life."*

The challenge is tremendous and we are

> *"His workmanship created in Christ Jesus unto good works, which He before has ordained that we should walk in them."*

"Holy Dippers" alone can faithfully transmit His truth (living water). Peter declared that "we are a Holy priesthood" and Paul said loud and clear that we are "called in Him to be Holy and blameless." God does not permit human adjustments of divine truths.

Paul instructed Timothy well when he wrote,

> *"Nevertheless, the firm foundation of God stands, having this seal, 'The Lord knows those who are His' and let everyone who names the name of the Lord abstain from wickedness. Therefore, if a man cleanses himself from these things, he will be a vessel for honor, sanctified, useful to the Master, prepared for every good work."*

I will never forget the old deep well with the crank and dipper I used as a child. How I loved to crank the bucket and drink from a dipper. How important that small vessel was to transmitting that cold crystal water on a hot, gnat-swarming day when my thirst was high and the well so deep. How privileged we are, as believer-pilgrims, believer-priests, believer-ambassadors, to be believer-dippers, of the water of life. The beauty of the dipper, the size of the dipper, the texture of the wood or metal of the dipper was never the issue, but always, "Is it clean?" and "Will it hold water?" God desires that we, who are His dippers, be clean vessels as we handle that precious water of life.

David said it well,

> "How shall a young man keep his way pure?" He does so "by keeping it according to Thy Word."

> "Thy word have I treasured in my heart, that I may not sin against Thee."

Jesus reminds us,

> "You are already clean because of the Word which I have spoken to you."

John emphasized the quality of that moment by moment fellowship that is cleansing and sure as he wrote,

"If we walk in the light, as He is in the light, we have fellowship with one another, and the blood of Jesus His Son cleanses us from all sin."

One would have to be absolutely blind spiritually to miss this truth that God has revealed for our lives. We have made it complex and difficult because we will not acknowledge our sins. As believers, if our lives are dirty and tainted it is our fellowship not our salvation that is affected; and the joy of our salvation is no longer because we are in disharmony and out of fellowship due to sin. Tombstones may speak their piece and we let what I say stand without challenge. Yet, we dare not be as the Pharisees who Jesus referred to as "whitened tombstones" that were filled with dead men's bones. The stakes are too high to be cute or curt.

When asked, "Who says?" we must well be able to answer as Peter commands us,

"But sanctify Christ as Lord in your hearts, always being ready to make a defense to everyone who asks you to give an account for the hope that is in you, yet with gentleness and reverence."

If we answer by any other authority, we are foolish. The failure of our lives to fulfill the believer-witness relationship or what we have termed the believer-dipper relationship is because we have not dealt honestly with our old sin nature that attracts the fleshy, like a dead thing draws flies. As a boy, I would have quickly discarded a "holey dipper" for it would have dribbled and run and the water would have been lost to my thirst. So it is with our lives as we are infected by sin and our "vitality drained away as with the intense heat of summer."

In the words of the old saints of the past we must "keep short accounts with God" remembering John's words,

> *"If we confess our sins, He is faithful and just to forgive our sins and cleanse us from all unrighteousness."*

We should try to remember always that clear formula of Paul's for living in the power of that crucified life. Remember from the first moment of our salvation until our last breath,

WE ARE IN SPIRITUAL WARFARE! BE ALERT!
Read Ephesians 6 Often!!!!

PAULS BATTLE PLAN

(1) Reckon ourselves dead to sin (Romans 6:11) – because of the finished work of Christ on our behalf

(2) Present not our body as an instrument to sin (Romans 6:13) – realizing that if we introduce ourselves to sin we will probably yield.

> *(3) Be filled with the Spirit (Ephesians 5:18) – therefore we will walk in the Spirit and not fulfill the lust of the flesh (Galatians 5:16)*

When we dare to trust God for such a radical walk, the truth of Psalm 32 is ours. We then become "holy dippers", vessels of privilege, which freely and joyfully carry the water of life. It was David who declared and we with him, the blessing of confessed sin and righteous living.

He wrote of God,

> *"Thou are my hiding place. Thou dost preserve me from trouble; Thou dost surround me with songs of deliverance (salvation). I will instruct you and teach you with my eye upon you."*

In this world where there are many voices making their pitch and bidding for our attention and affection we must seek to tune our lives to eternal truth alone as our authority and hope. Men may attack and equate their philosophies with God's truth, but we must not be moved. Our debating and argument is called futile by Scripture.

Paul reminded Timothy,

> *"Remind them of these things, and solemnly charge them in the presence of God not to wrangle about*

words, this is useless and leads to the ruin of the hearers."

Ultimately, the proof of all proofs is the changed life that is produced by grace, supernaturally given.

George Sym says concerning this reality,

> *"The evidence of a transformed life has no rebuttal. Men have tried countless ways to change others for the better. Both punishment and rehabilitation have failed. Often, education only teaches cleverer ways to do wrong and get away with it. But the influence of one who really demonstrates a changed life is irresistible. A group of preachers were once comparing Bible translations when one said, 'My favorite translation and the one which made me a minster is the way my mother translated the gospel by living it'."*

As a pilgrim-believer, we often become weary of the many false signs of "They said" or "He said" along life's road, but we must ever,

> *"Look unto Jesus the author and finisher of our faith, who for the joy set before Him endured the cross despising the shame and has sat down at the right hand of the throne of God."*

CHAPTER 21

WHAT'S THE ANSWER?

The proclamation of the "evangel," the good news of Christ's death, burial and resurrection, is a supernatural message. We who proclaim that message are also the results of a supernatural work of grace. We are indeed the work of God proclaiming and giving witness to the living Word of God.

There are many times in our lives that we do not comprehend all that God is saying to us. There are times when His leading is beyond our human rationale. I have had to learn for myself over a long period of time that "the secret things belong to the Lord our God, but the things revealed belong to us and to our sons forever."

How precious to my life has been the learning process by which I have come to know that God's Word alone is that rock upon which I stand. All that He has revealed for my growing, going and giving is therein revealed.

I can surely testify with David,

"How sweet are Thy words to my taste! Yes, sweeter than honey to the mouth! From Thy precepts I get understanding; therefore I hate every false way."

The questions about life are right, the answers are certain. God has promised to us as He promised to Jeremiah,

"Thus says the Lord, who made the earth, the Lord who formed it to establish it, the Lord is His name, call to Me and I will answer you, and I will tell you great and mighty things, which you do not know."

God's truth is given by supernatural revelation to those "who seek" Him as His Spirit acts upon their lives. The work of evangelism is the work of God. As His witnesses, we are commissioned and enabled by God for this work. David was referred to by God as "a man after His own heart." Even with his tragic sins, he was a man of contrite heart.

If we are to be those faithful vessels that are used of God, we must learn to walk in fellowship with God and man with contrite hearts and humble spirits. In so doing, the Spirit of God will teach us His truth as we declare His Name to our world. **We live by FAITH not Feeling always KNOWING what we feel not Feeling what we KNOW! KNOW GOD'S WORD!**

Isaiah spoke to the matter of a contrite heart, humble spirit and God's Word!

> *"For My hand made all these things, thus all these things came into being, declares the Lord. But to this one will I look, to him who is humble and contrite of spirit and who trembles at My Word."*

Our greatest ministry in evangelism is not the giving of answers, but the raising of proper questions in the minds of the on-looking world, as God, through our daily witness seeks to save those who are lost. Only from a contrite heart comes the blessing of God upon our lives. There has been a tendency these days to externalize evangelism and our relationship with God to the point that they have become productions. We are more often a more self-righteous Pharisee than a contrite believer-witness walking in a humble connection with God before man.

We were commanded by Paul the apostle to make it our ambition to:

> *"Live a quiet life, mind our own business and work with our hands."*

Peter also declared that we should,

> *"...be ready to give a reason of the hope that is in us, to those that asked."*

We must cease being aggressors but servants in the matter of evangelism. Truly, "Ambassadorial Evangelism" is for those who ask.

George Verwer said it well when he wrote,

> "Outward marks are often deceptive. The clever Christian, the one who excels in fluent praying or vigorous preaching, or the one who can answer all theological questions, is not necessarily a disciple. Nor is it necessarily the one who has sold everything down to his last shirt, an act of "true discipleship". These things of themselves do not draw us close to God. But God draws near and the Scripture says, "unto them that are of a broken heart and saveth them that are of a contrite spirit." While we seek honor for ourselves, or try to advance the program or reputation of the movement or a preacher, we are building on the fragile merit of men. As the mark of a true disciple is his hunger for God, his goal is God's approval. His counsel remains, "Be still and know that I am God." (Psalms 46:10) The only way to find the necessary power of resources for each day is to quietly wait on God. Plan time to be alone with Him. Learn to delight in Him. Cultivate a hunger for his infinite being. Without this, your work will be superficial; with it your deepest desires will be filled and your discipleship will glorify Him."

The ultimate answer to evangelizing our world is a commitment of life and life style of each believer to the Lordship of Christ. Evangelizing the world does not mean converting every person on planet Earth, but rather giving all of mankind an opportunity to hear the Good News of Jesus Christ. As believers, we have no choice about whether we will choose to be a disciple-witness for our salvation has declared it to be a necessity. We, in the relationship, may prove either faithful or unfaithful, but we are witnesses nevertheless.

Elton Trueblood put it this way,

> *"It is in the general setting of the necessity of giving witness and the consequent fellowship of witness that the famous doctrine of universal priesthood of all believers begins to come alive. All Christians must be in the ministry, whatever their occupations, because the non-witnessing follower of Christ is a contradiction in terms. If we take seriously Christ's first group order, the command to let our light shine, we dare not let the witness be limited to a small group of professionally religious. Therefore, the ministry of Christ must be universal. It must be universal in three specific ways. It must involve "all places", it must involve "all times", and it must involve "all Christian persons," male and female, lay and clerical, old and young."*

The believer and the church must become radical in the matters of the Word and the "Spirit." Hype cannot produce this nor can programs or activities, as good as they may be. The energies of the flesh are just great "methodeia," that is, natural rather than supernatural.

It is an overwhelming challenge knowing human nature as we do, but it is not impossible to know God as we do! With the ingredients of a faithful, knowledgeable, studying teacher-pastor, player-coach or elder and a flock of a few or many, this discipleship becomes a reality. It matters not whether a ministry is large or small but a determined faithfulness and a consistent, orderly study of God's Word will grow a disciple.

Thus, the true picture of the "church" would emerge; and we with the spiritual, social and intellectual aspects of our faith as commissioned, would be brought under discipleship. This is the answer; but knowing as we do the weaknesses of the flesh, it is radical! Each and every believer-pilgrim-priest-ambassador-witness must faithfully share together GOD'S WORD with brothers and sisters in Christ if they are to grow in grace!

David said,

> "Behold, how good and how pleasant it is for brothers to dwell together in unity!"

This unity is only achieved as we submit to one another in love, giving each other over to God to direct and build each one in that "most holy faith." **THIS IS ANNOTHERING!** The evangelizing of the world has as much to do with the functioning of the community of believers as with the individual witnesses. The gathered body of believers is commissioned to reflect God's love in their dealings with one another.

Dietrich Bonhoeffer writes,

> *"Therefore spiritual love proves itself in that everything it says and does commends Christ. It will not seek to move others y all too personal, direct influence, by impure interference in the life of another. It will not take pleasure in pious, human fervor and excitement. It will rather meet the other person with the clear Word of God and be ready to leave him alone with the Word of God and be ready to leave him alone again in order that Christ may deal with him. It will respect the line that has been drawn between him and us by Christ, and it will find full fellowship with him in the Christ who alone binds us together. Thus, this spiritual love will speak to Christ about a brother, more than to a brother about Christ. It knows that the most direct way to others is always through prayer to Christ and that love of others is wholly dependent upon the truth in Christ. It is of this love that John the disciple speaks, "I have no greater joy than to hear that my children walk in the truth."*

Each believer must understand who they are before God. The Bible reveals that all believers stand before God equally. Our corporate relationship is known as the "communion of the saints," which allows us to share in that "heavenly fellowship" here and now. God has intended that through the "love of the brethren" all men would know that "we are His disciples."

True evangelism depends not only on the personal witness of each believer but is also dependent upon a bold, loving corporate witness. A great force for evangelism in any community is a loving fellowship of believers whose love is driven by God's love and grace not a sentimental self-serving love.

Perhaps the most important link in the chain of ministry that will produce this reality is the faithful, knowledgeable teaching and studying of God's Word in small groups. Large crowds can hear the gospel and be impregnated by the truth, but will need small interactive gatherings for discipleship. It is necessary to question answers and answer questions. There are no bad questions, only bad answers!

Such men who will elevate and magnify the Scriptures above "all else" will not only introduce maturity to people but will also stabilize their lives in this cosmetic, superficial, fleshy world. "The equipping of the saints for the work of the ministry," can, in God's time and according to God's plan, become a spiritual reality in the life of any ministry.

How sad it is that often in our eagerness for the harvest of evangelism that we have failed to see that we must tend to the root of evangelism if we are to know the "fruit" of evangelism. If we fail here in instructing and edifying the believer-disciple-witness we will never evangelize our world. Gimmicks and programs are not needed. They might motivate for a while, but they externalize truth more than internalize it. In time they will retard rather than develop true biblical evangelism and will encourage shallow discipleship.

There is nothing as healthy as a loving and Word-centered flock of believers who believe God and submit themselves to His truth and to each other in love. The larger a ministry grows, the more responsible it is to add other teaching elders and /or pastors to meet the individual spiritual needs of the whole flock, whether young or old, rich or poor. God will always give the increase; for He has promised and He cannot, nor will He not lie.

Isaiah spoke this truth as he declared God's promise,

"My Word which goes forth from my mouth; it shall not return to Me empty, without accomplishing what I desire, and without succeeding in the matter for which I sent it."

The greatest megaphone for the telling of the Gospel is not radio, television or any other media, but the faithful witness of a single changed life that impacts another, who in turn impacts another and on and on. To be sure, the media is not in and of itself evil, but we have often in our time allowed it to dominate our thinking because the world does. Talking heads and faceless crowds may be evangelized, but not discipled. To be sure, there are many occasions when we should use whatever media is available to give witness to the truth. But we must never lose the dynamic of the one to one proclamation, for it is here that Biblical evangelism is all that God intended it to be.

Trueblood writes,

"Somewhere in the world, there should be a society consciously and deliberately devoted to the task of seeing how love can be made real and demonstrating love in practice. Unfortunately, there is really only one candidate for this task. If God, as we believe, is truly revealed in the life of Christ, the most important thing to Him is the creation of centers of loving fellowship, which is to infect the world."

This is the church at her best!

We contemporary believers believe a lie when we believe that to do a "great" work for God when we must always magnify our image or voice by some mechanical means. Our greatest witness is that "witness" that faithfully declares God's Word and allows His Spirit to do the simplifying. Throughout history God has always amplified that simple witness or act of faith and trust, thereby changing lives. It is time that we get on with the task realizing that the Apostle Paul evangelized a great part of the civilized world of his day by faithfully communicating the truth within the providence of God for his life. This same reality can be true in "our world" of activity and routine as we live faithfully within the providence of God for us. It must be said once again that the use of media of any kind is not in itself sinful; but it can become a fad. We see ministries today that once used the media to advantage, but now the media controls how they minister.

Many have fallen into a pattern of "monkey see-monkey do." Ministries and men have sought to copy some unique person or ministry that may be ordained for a special task. A special kind of ministry may not be the rule, but rather the exception. There is even an idea insinuated of not having done "our best" to evangelize our world if we don't have the complete conglomeration of media ministries. This is indeed tragic! Perhaps we have become media dependent and should concentrate instead on that precious one to one communication that was ordained by God when He sought Adam and Eve in the cool of the day.

The greatest ministry in the entire world is still the ministry of warm loving bodies, "temples of the Holy Spirit," who dare to share God's message face to face. True instruction and ministry demands that we come together to be stimulated to love and good deeds. Electronic and media images can never do this even at their best, nor can talking heads and faceless crowds.

Perhaps we have become practical atheists who speak much of God and His truths but whose lives are little affected. The true believer has been given new life and that life will not be denied even in its infant form. Charles Templeton who has long since moved away from his evangelical beginnings, addresses us most prophetically when he included in his book the following insights,

> *"The church is a cherished institution, but (while there are, of course, notable exceptions) it wields little direct influence upon the thinking of millions within its membership. All too frequently, Christians who readily*

admit the existence of God, deny His Lordship in practice. Much of the atheism of our time is unconscious, unargued and implicit. The average church member has little grasp of the faith he espouses. Though natively religious, Americans are religiously illiterate. Many a church member matures in every area of life except the religious, continuing to hold concepts about the nature and will of God learned in childhood. We have grown soft in prosperity. Our membership rolls are fat, our buildings are luxurious, our endowments seem to secure the future, and our faith finds general approval. One would not disparage achievement or betray a guilt complex by lusting after persecution, but there is a danger that the Church will not so much convert the world as be converted by the world to its way of life. Living too close to society and not daring to condemn with too great a vigor the sins to which it is itself given, the Church stands in danger that the time will come when (to paraphrase G.K. Chesterton) it can pick up a microphone and address the entire world only to find it has nothing to say. Christianity is not a matter of making a single 'decision for Christ'; it is a whole life of decision. The command is to 'take up their cross daily'; and one carries the cross through new territory in every state of the Christian pilgrimage. Men must constantly be called to continual commitment and to the dedication of new areas of their lives. This too is evangelism."

If anything is clear, it is that there are outstanding opportunities today for Biblical, Spirit-led evangelism.

Even for the most inconspicuous believer, life's routine under the Spirit's leadership will provide significant opportunities. Yet, as always, there are many adversaries. There are many spiritual frontiers to be conquered. The greatest of them all is our own flesh. Victory can be ours! God has given us His grace, His Spirit and his Word (promises); so we are not alone. There is no excuse for holding back.

We do not have to live defeated, carnal, shallow lives of constant broken fellowship with God and man. He is our victory!

Jude declared:

> *"Now to Him who is able to keep you from stumbling and to make you stand in the presence of His glory, blameless with great joy, to the only God our Savior, through Jesus Christ our Lord, be glory, majesty, dominion and authority, before all them now and forever. Amen"*

I recall a soliloquy that I once read and it went something like this,

Jesus hid within a book

Isn't worth a second look.

Jesus buried in a creed,

Is a helpless Christ indeed!

But Jesus in the hearts of men,

Shows his saving pow'r again.

We are indeed believer-pilgrim-priest-ambassador-evangelists, "holy dippers," and earthen vessels by which the water of life, the Gospel of our Lord Jesus Christ, is to be proclaimed to the ends of the earth. There is an answer! WE ARE IT! WE are winners, for God's promise is sure,

> *"Being confident of this very thing, that He that has begun a good work in you will perform it until the day of Jesus Christ." (Philippians 1:6)*

Faithful witnessing of the Gospel before a watching world is our task and now is the time.

The words of an old proverb state this beautifully,

> *"We are the ones and if not us, Who?*
>
> *Now is the time and if not now, When?"*

> *"Therefore, my beloved brethren, be steadfast, immovable, always abounding in the work of the Lord, knowing that our toil is not in vain in the Lord."*

THE MOMENT WE TRUST JESUS CHRIST

GOD'S PROVISION

I became a child of God – John 1:12

I was chosen of God and born by His will – Ephesians 1:2, John 1:13

My sins past, present and future were forgiven – Romans 4:7-8, 2 Corinthians 5;21

I became an heir of God and joint heir with Jesus Christ – Romans 5:9

I was saved from the wrath of God – Romans 5:9

I was reckoned righteous – Romans 4,5,6

I received eternal life – John 5:24, I John 5:13

I was guaranteed no condemnation – John 5:24, Romans 8:1

I was reconciled to God – 2 Corinthians 5:18

I was justified and given peace with God – Romans 5:1-2

I was born again of incorruptible seed – I Peter 1:23

I was delivered from the power of darkness and redeemed – Colossians 1:13-14

I was made a new creation, now in Christ forever – 2 Corinthians 5:17

I was sanctified and perfected forever – I Corinthians 1:30, Hebrews 10:10, 14

I have been made complete in Christ – Colossians 2:8-15

I was born of the Spirit, my body is His temple – John 3:16, I Corinthians 6:19-20

I was baptized in the Holy Spirit – I Corinthians 12:13

I was indwelt by the Holy Spirit – John 14:16-17, Romans 8:9

I was sealed by the Holy Spirit – Ephesians 1:13-14, 4:30

I became a citizen of heaven – Ephesians 2:19, Philippians 3:20

I am His workmanship – Ephesians 2:20

I am made able to walk in the newness of life – Romans 6:4

I am no longer a forced slave of sin – Romans 6:6-7

I was the recipient of God's free gift – Romans 6:23, Ephesians 2:8-9

I was enabled to bear fruit for God – Romans 7:4

I was enabled to serve in the newness of Spirit – Romans 7:6

I was set free from the law of sin and death – Romans 8:2

I was enabled to please God – Romans 8:5-9

I now belong to Christ and was made spiritually alive in Him – Romans 8:9-10

I am unable to be separated from the love of God – Romans 8:35-39

GRACE'S LIFESTYLE

"ONE anothering"

Be devoted to ONE another ... Romans 12:10

Give preference to ONE another... Romans 12:10

Be of the same mind toward ONE another...Romans 12:16

Love ONE another...Romans 13:8

Accept ONE another...Romans 15:7

Admonish ONE another...Romans 15:14

Care for ONE another...I Corinthians 12:25

Serve ONE another...Galatians 5:13

Bear ONE another's burdens...Galatians 6:2

Show patience to ONE another...Ephesians 4:1-2

Be kind to ONE another...Ephesians 4:32

Do not lie to ONE another...Colossians 3:9

Bear with ONE another...Colossians 3:12-13

Teach and admonish ONE another...Colossians 3:16

Comfort ONE another...I Thessalonians 4:18

Encourage ONE another...Hebrews 3:13

Stimulate ONE another to love and good deeds...Hebrews 10:23

Pray for ONE another...James 5:16

Do not speak against ONE another...James 4:11

Do not complain...against ONE another...James 5:9

IN MAJOR MATTERS UNITY
IN MINOR MATTERS FREEDOM
IN ALL MATTERS CHARITY

MANIFEST HUMILITY TO ALL
IN A HURTING WORLD
IN JESUS NAME

JESUS NOT ME-SUS!!!

OTHER WORKS BY DANNY GRIFFIN

- **<u>Dancing With Broken Feet</u>**
  Dealing with the pain and pressures of marriage including divorce, remarriage, blended families and more

- **<u>Dancing With A Broken World</u>**
  Danny takes his knowledge from decades of walking with the Lord and weds Biblical truth with practical living.

- **<u>Dancing With Jesus In A Hurting World</u>**
  Danny uplifts and encourages the true believer and follower of Christ to be God's ambassadorial mission in today's culture and world.

- **<u>Dancing With Amazing Grace</u>** (coming soon)
  The word GRACE is used 159 times in Scripture. Danny defines and explores this astounding concept.

- **<u>Dancing With A Broken Me</u>** (coming soon)
  Danny personalizes his walk with the LORD and strives to answer the question, "Who are you really, pilgrim?"

For information on how to obtain any of the above visit:
<u>http://www.SpiritualMaintenance.org/Books.html</u>

CPSIA information can be obtained
at www.ICGtesting.com
Printed in the USA
FFHW01n2200110918
48352854-52188FF